EXAM REVISION

AS/A-LEVEL

Media Studies

David Probert

Philip Allan Updates
Market Place
Deddington
Oxfordshire
OX15 0SE

Orders

Bookpoint Ltd, 130 Milton Park, Abingdon, Oxfordshire, OX14 4SB
tel: 01235 827720
fax: 01235 400454
e-mail: uk.orders@bookpoint.co.uk
Lines are open 9.00 a.m.–5.00 p.m., Monday to Saturday, with a 24-hour message
answering service. You can also order through the Philip Allan Updates website:
www.philipallan.co.uk

ISBN-13: 978-0-86003-449-0
ISBN-10: 0-86003-449-6

Cover illustration by John Spencer
Printed in Spain

Philip Allan Updates' policy is to use papers that are natural, renewable and recyclable
products and made from wood grown in sustainable forests. The logging and
manufacturing processes are expected to conform to the environmental regulations
of the country of origin.

Contents

Introduction 1
 1 About this book 1
 2 How to use these notes 1
 3 How to revise 2
 4 The AQA, OCR and WJEC specifications 3
 5 Assessment objectives in A-level media studies 4
 6 Differences between AS and A2 5
 7 Your approach to media studies 5

Chapter 1 Key concepts in media studies
 1 The key concepts explained 7
  1.1 Genre 7
  1.2 Representation 8
  1.3 Audience 8
  1.4 Values and ideology 9
  1.5 Institutions 9
  1.6 Language 11
 2 Applying the key concepts to text analysis 12
  2.1 Questions to be considered (AS/A2) 12
 3 Wider contexts and the analysis of media texts (A2) 15
  3.1 Social contexts 16
  3.2 Historical contexts 19
  3.3 Economic contexts 27
  3.4 Political contexts 28

Chapter 2 Moving image text analysis
 1 Specification focus: AQA Unit 1 (AS) 31
 2 Specification focus: AQA Unit 6 (A2) 31
 3 Technical aspects of the moving image 33
  3.1 Camera angle 33
  3.2 Other film terminology 34
  3.3 Editing 34
  3.4 Sound 35
  3.5 Special effects/graphics 35
  3.6 Mise-en-scène 35
 4 Semiology and text analysis (AS/A2) 35
  4.1 Terminology and principles 35
  4.2 Classification and characteristics of signs 36
  4.3 Organisation and combination of signs 36

4.4 Application of semiotics to cultural artefacts 36

4.5 Useful words in semiotics 37

4.6 Application of semiology to the visual image 38

Chapter 3 Textual topics and analysis

1 Specification focus: OCR Unit 2731 (AS), Section B 39

   1.1 Consumerism and lifestyle magazines 39

   1.2 Celebrity and the tabloid press 40

   1.3 Music culture and radio 42

   1.4 Gender and television situation comedy 44

2 Specification focus: AQA Unit 2 (AS) 44

   2.1 Film and broadcast fiction 45

   2.2 Documentary 46

   2.3 Advertising and marketing 48

   2.4 British newspapers 51

Chapter 4 Texts and contexts in the media

1 Specification focus: AQA Unit 4 (A2) 63

   1.1 The production and manufacture of news 63

   1.2 Representations 67

   1.3 Genre 73

   1.4 Media audiences 78

2 Specification focus: OCR Unit 2732 (AS) 84

Chapter 5 Media issues and debates

1 Specification focus: OCR Unit 2735 (A2) 85

   1.1 Broadcasting 85

   1.2 Film 90

   1.3 Print 93

Introduction

About this book

Media studies is not like most other academic subjects, with their fixed body of knowledge to be learned and included in examination answers. It is student-centred and focused on the individual student's consumption of media texts and on his or her responses to those texts, expressed within a framework of media concepts and terminology.

The range of texts to be studied under the different specifications is wide, and a set of revision notes cannot attempt to cover them in any detail. It is the methodology of analysing texts, and the economic, social and cultural contexts of their construction and consumption, that are dealt with in these notes. A thorough understanding of these methodologies should allow you to deconstruct, analyse and explore any media products.

In these revision notes you will find definitions and explanations of these approaches, together with the key terminology and techniques involved in dissecting, analysing and evaluating media texts and the part they play in our lives. Media studies is concerned with the production, marketing and consumption of media texts and the ways in which they represent and embody the attitudes, beliefs and values of the world in which we live.

Regardless of the various media effects debates (which argue to what degree we are shaped by media versions of the world), there can be little doubt that whether we are watching the news on the BBC, MTV, al-Jazeera, CNN or Fox, or watching a Disney cartoon or *Sex in the City*, the agendas, representations, attitudes, beliefs, values and ideologies expressed through media products form an important part of our socialisation and help to shape our personal identity and generate our expectations of life.

As individuals, we are totally dependent on media representations for knowledge of the world beyond our immediate experience. Studying the media involves recognising and exploring these representations, and understanding their sources and the motivations of those who construct them. A knowledge of media processes empowers individuals by helping them to develop their own critical autonomy and an informed, challenging approach to media texts.

Students of the media should prepare themselves by developing a wide interest in current affairs and global issues and by scanning the national press and watching television on a daily basis to provide background contexts to media debates.

How to use these notes

Media studies requires an active, well-informed, articulate student who uses appropriate vocabulary and concepts to explore media industries and texts. These notes are designed to refresh memories, sharpen intellect and equip you for this exploration.

Examples are provided to help explain the process, but as every media course is approached slightly differently and involves the use of different texts, these can never reflect all of the materials used in a course. These notes provide brief reminders of key terminology and approaches to the various elements of the subject and should be used in conjunction with textbooks, prepared case studies and other materials.

The subject is approached through the media **key concepts**, which should be applied in any analysis or discussion of media texts.

Media studies examination specifications are offered by AQA, OCR and the Welsh Joint Education Committee (WJEC). Although broadly covering the same ground, the specifications and units are presented differently. The contents of these notes are relevant to all three specifications and the key concept terminology applies to any study of the media. Specific reference is made throughout to AQA or OCR units and the descriptive terminology is adapted in line with the different approaches taken by these two specifications. In some areas, questions and answers are used to help develop approaches to the topic.

It is important to remember that these notes are designed for examination-based units and that coursework units are not covered. Guidance on coursework for some AQA and OCR units can be found in the *Student Unit Guides* also published by Philip Allan Updates.

How to revise

- Plan your revision well ahead of the date of the examination.
- Note down the exam dates (specifying exact times).
- Make sure of the content of each exam and the format of the exam paper.
- Plan revision for each paper in turn.
- Look at past papers and use these exam revision notes as the basis for your revision.
- Make sure that you cover all of the topics that may form part of the examination.
- Find out what revision routine suits your personality and learning style.
- Raise any problems or difficulties you have with your teacher.
- Be sure to attend any revision classes, and during these make notes and ask questions.

Do not:
- leave everything until the last minute
- avoid revising difficult topics
- stop taking recreation time — you need proper breaks from revision schedules
- cram all night before an exam — you will be too tired to think properly

On the day:
- make a check list of everything you need (you should prepare this the night before the exam)
- eat well at breakfast time
- be sure of the exam's location
- give yourself plenty of time to arrive, allowing for traffic and delays
- take some bottled water with you and chew something if it helps you to relax and concentrate
- stay calm — breathe slowly and deeply if you feel anxious

In the exam room:
- fill in all of the required details on the front of your answer book
- read all instructions carefully, ensuring that you know how many questions to answer and from which choices

- skim the whole paper before starting
- allocate time appropriately to all questions and be careful not to get carried away by your favourite topic
- read through the paper
- make a brief plan of your answers, but don't waste too much time
- keep glancing at the question and refer to key elements in your answer
- don't revert to prepared answers that do not address the question
- pace yourself, and stay within time constraints you have set
- never leave the exam early — there is always some correction or addition you can make
- spend any time at the end of the exam rereading your answers

The AQA, OCR and WJEC specifications

Media studies is a broad-based subject and the specifications produced by AQA, OCR and WJEC approach the same topics in slightly different ways, sometimes using different terminology. For ease of comparison, the titles of all the units are listed below.

AQA

AQA has six modules, all of which emphasise the application of key concepts:

AS

1 Reading the media
2 Textual topics in contemporary media
3 Practical production (coursework, so not covered in these notes)

A2

4 Texts and contexts in the media
5 Independent study (coursework, so not covered in these notes)
6 Comparative critical analysis

OCR

OCR has six units, two of which are practical and two of which involve case study materials.

AS

2730 Foundation production (coursework, so not covered in these notes)
2731 Textual analysis
2732 Case study: audiences and institutions (not covered in detail by these notes)

A2

2733 Advanced production (coursework, so not covered in these notes)
2734 Critical research study (case study materials provided by the examining board)
2735 Media issues and debates

Welsh Joint Education Committee (WJEC)

WJEC has six units, two of which are coursework:

AS

1 Modern media forms
2 Media representations and reception
3 Making media texts (practical)

A2

4 Investigating media texts (coursework)
5 Changing media industries
6 Text and context

These notes provide terminology and content applicable to all the examination-based elements. The specific texts (and, in some cases, the approach adopted by centres to the subject matter) may differ.

Assessment objectives in A-level media studies

Assessment objectives are the skills you must demonstrate if you are to succeed in A-level media studies. These include your knowledge and understanding of the subject or topic and your ability to evaluate content and write analytically.

The assessment objectives in media studies are ranged across the six assessment units for the AQA and OCR specifications, with some relating specifically to the coursework studies that are not covered in these notes.

The principal focus of assessment for media studies is knowledge and application of the key concepts; at A2, a wider awareness of social, historical, economic and political contexts is required.

Although the assessment objectives are expressed differently by AQA and OCR, they cover broadly the same ground and are similar to those of WJEC. The emphasis in the AQA specification is on an approach using media studies key concepts that, although present in the OCR specification, are not identified as such. The WJEC specification is not referenced in these notes, although much of the content is covered.

AQA assessment objectives

You must demonstrate your knowledge, application and evaluation of:
● texts and ideas, using the key concepts
● wider social, historical, economic and political contexts within which media texts are produced (A2 only)
● at least one media technology (this applies to the AS practical Unit 3)
● ideas, theories, debates and information concerning contemporary media
● a range of contemporary texts, exploring their similarities and differences

You must also demonstrate use of investigative research techniques, through an independent study of media texts, topics or issues (this applies to coursework Unit 5)

OCR assessment objectives

At AS you must:
● understand how meaning is constructed through the use of specific media language
● demonstrate knowledge and understanding of media institutions, technologies, production processes and audiences, and apply this knowledge to the consumption and reception of media texts
● show an understanding of how social groups are represented and how they represent themselves in the media, comparing messages, values and social signification in media texts
● plan and construct a media text from a prescribed brief, demonstrating technical skill and understanding of audience representation, genre and form (Unit 2730 — practical)

- record, monitor and evaluate the process of production from planning to outcome, using appropriate media terminology (Unit 2730 — practical)

At A2 you must:

- use appropriate investigative and critical techniques to independently research and analyse a media topic, and present findings
- develop critical arguments about media issues and debates, evaluating contemporary theories and applying knowledge to texts
- originate and construct an original media text from a brief, demonstrating technical skill and an understanding of audience, genre, representation and form (Unit 2733 — practical)
- critically analyse the process and outcome of the production, drawing on knowledge of media institutions, audiences and theories (Unit 2733 — practical)

Differences between AS and A2

It is important to remember that your skills are developing and accumulating as you complete the various units of your course. The last unit, taken at the end of the course, is always intended to be **synoptic**, meaning that it is designed to assess your overall progression and the skills and knowledge you have developed during your course and in completing the other units. A2 units are also designed to show your understanding of the **wider contexts** involved in the production of media texts. While some units involve the display of specific knowledge of media content and theory, all units involve the use of the key concepts as the basic tools of media analysis.

The key concept approach provides a clear and comprehensive basis for approaching all media texts in all three specifications and is used as the focus of these notes.

Important terms and definitions are shown in **bold** to attract attention and for ease of reference. 'Examiner's tips' and 'Ideas for application' are provided to help you understand how to approach the subject.

Your approach to media studies

These notes have had to strike a balance between length, detail and accessibility. If they were too long they would just become another textbook and that would defeat the object of providing easy reference and clear outlines of key areas.

Media studies is a text-based subject and the number and range of possible texts that could be used as source material is vast and yet still may not include the actual texts studied in your centre.

One problem is the immediacy factor so important in media texts. Texts are conceived, produced and consumed as part of a dynamic creative cycle. Part of their appeal is their newness and the buzz of attraction around their appearance and their content. Some become classics and are continually referenced, for example the original Volkswagen Beetle car ads, the Levis 501 campaign of the 1980s or classic films like *Citizen Kane*, but even films are subject to adaptation and 'remakes', to alter and enhance their appeal for a new generation.

Nobody wants yesterday's news or yesterday's newspapers but we all want a glimpse of tomorrow's. How often have you scanned 'new' media textbooks only to be amused at their dated examples, forgotten and irrelevant scandals and controversies? This is the reason that one of the best texts to be used in any media course is always that morning's national newspapers. Examples in media studies, then, are only illustrative. What you must do is apply the principles explained to fresh examples of your own. Watch films, buy magazines and read newspapers! These are your best examples.

You should not be disappointed if you do not find the particular texts you have studied during your course analysed in these notes. Understanding media approaches, processes, contexts, terminology and the key concepts is far more important and should allow you to analyse and explore any media text you are asked to consider with confidence. Remember, the examiner is looking for your personal consumption of the media and the critical autonomy you display in assessing media issues against a background of knowledge.

Your views must be based on a clear understanding of the theories, context and issues relating to media representations of the world, and if you express your knowledge with enthusiasm and demonstrate an engagement with media issues you should achieve your objective of examination success.

CHAPTER 1 *Key concepts in media studies*

This chapter covers the key concepts — essential tools for AS and A2 media studies courses. The AS year usually begins with an outline of the key concepts and their application to media texts. These concepts are the basis of any analysis of the media and any discussion or evaluation of media topics involves their use. As listed below, they form the acronym GRAVIL and form a useful check list for examination purposes:

- **G**enre
- **R**epresentation
- **A**udience
- **V**alues and ideology
- **I**nstitutions
- **L**anguage

The key concepts explained

1.1 Genre

This term defines a category, style or type of media product.

Why is genre important?

Classification of texts into genres seems to be a natural part of making sense of the cultural world. Children as young as five can classify television programmes and distinguish them by identifying key generic features, such as recognising real or pretend violence. Identifying genres helps audiences to make sense of plot conventions and narrative structures.

- All media products can be categorised as belonging to genres.
- Genres are identified by the repetition of distinctive features.
- Genres can be divided into sub-genres, for example vampire horror is a sub-genre of horror.
- Genres can determine the narrative conventions of a text.
- Genres generate expectations in audiences.
- Genres are used by producers to structure media products.

How can we identify a genre?

Genres can usually be identified through the sharing of common:

- character types
- iconography
- plots
- props
- locations
- music and soundtracks
- narratives or storylines

EXAMINER'S TIP

The difference between a plot and storyline is that the plot involves the technical means by which the audience is given information about the narrative progression of a film or drama. This can include camera movement, shot type and the soundtrack that accompanies the action, which are used to explain the motivation of characters and their progress through the time frame of the action. The storyline is the story that is being told.

1.2 Representation

This is the process whereby the media construct versions of people, places and events in images, words or sound for transmission through media texts to audiences. Representation is the basis of all media products. We live our lives through actual experience of others and the world around us. Media products construct versions of the living experience through representations.

- Representations provide models of how we see gender, social groups and places — aspects of the world we all inhabit.
- They are ideological in that they are constructed within a framework of values and beliefs.
- They are **mediated** by individuals and media organisations and reflect the value systems of their sources.
- No representations are real; they are only versions of the real.

> **Mediation:** the means by which, through the use of representation, a media organisation and its employees stand between an event and the public's perception of that event. The constructed versions of people, places and events that result in media representations involve changes to those people, places and events.

1.3 Audience

Audiences are the groups of individuals targeted by producers as the intended consumers of media texts.

Why is the study of audiences important?

All media products assume the existence of an audience. The identification of an audience is vital for media producers, as this will affect the contents of the media text. The responses of audiences — **audience positioning** — can be researched and predicted as part of the process of marketing media texts. Audiences are affected in some way by media texts and the nature of this is the basis for a wide range of media research. Because of the wide availability of these texts, the actual viewers, readers or listeners may not always be those originally intended.

How are audiences defined?

Audiences are traditionally defined according to a system of social classification used by advertisers and researchers:

A   professional workers: lawyers, doctors, managers of large organisations
B   shopkeepers, farmers, teachers, white-collar workers
C1   skilled manual high grade: builders, carpenters, shop assistants, nurses
C2   skilled manual low grade: electricians, plumbers
D   semi-skilled manual: bus drivers, lorry drivers, fitters
E   unskilled manual: general labourers, bartenders, porters

The scale is used to classify media audiences and to distinguish between the readership of tabloid and quality newspapers. The system has drawbacks as it ignores the class that people may think they belong to. In addition, social status does not necessarily relate to financial status, income, patterns of spending or aspirations. (For further discussion of audience classification, see the section on Advertising and marketing on p. 48.)

EXAMINER'S TIP

Although audiences are targeted by media producers, easy access and the open nature of media texts mean that there is often no way of ensuring that only the target audience accesses the product. For example, unless encrypted systems are used on television channels and strict controls are applied to the sale of magazines, children can access material aimed at adults. Although a certification system applies to videos and DVDs for sale or rental, there is evidence that children and young people under the specified age frequently gain access to adult material

1.4 Values and ideology

Ideology consists of a set of attitudes, beliefs and values held in common by a group of people and culturally produced within a community to sustain a particular way of life. Values and ideology are part of every media text. Understanding their presence is essential in order to explain how media texts influence us and the world that we inhabit.

- Religions such as Islam and Christianity and **meta discourses** such as **Marxism** are ideologies.
- All media products have an ideological dimension to them and are constructed within the context of a dominant ideology or a series of common sense values that are generally shared and understood by all members of a community.
- Marxists see these values as representing the interests of the dominant or ruling class and their maintenance of power.

Ideology is present in all media texts. It can be explored by assessing the attitudes, beliefs and values embedded within a text. Assumptions made about how the viewer or reader thinks and feels can be analysed.

TERMINOLOGY

Meta discourse: a postmodernist term used to describe all-embracing social theories like Marxism, which claim to provide a scientific framework for explaining how societies work.
Marxism: an ideology derived from the writings of the sociologist Karl Marx (1818–83), which sees society as dominated by capitalist structures that maintain the dominance of the ruling class and lead to the exploitation of workers. Marx's analysis sees the world dominated by 'class struggle', resulting in the eventual triumph of the working class through a process of revolutionary change. Marx's ideology forms the basis of belief in communist states and is still advocated by political parties throughout the world.

EXAMINER'S TIP

It is important to see the underlying ideology behind everyday assumptions in media texts, especially as the 'common sense' nature of ideology sometimes makes it seem invisible. A soap powder advertisement, showing two women discussing how to get the cleanest wash and which product to use, is ideological in that it assumes that women do the washing. It also makes assumptions that having clean washing carries social status and that knowledge of a particular product can help achieve this status.

1.5 Institutions

Institutions are collections of individuals working together in a hierarchical structure to achieve clearly defined, shared goals. Most will be business organisations — often part of large corporations working to achieve profitable financial returns on investments.

Some institutions may be set up by governments, with a specific function defined by law, but these too will have clear objectives and achievement targets, usually defined in financial terms.

Why are institutions important?

Institutions determine and constrain the ideology, structure, content and distribution of media texts and are involved in the regulation and control of those texts. Nearly all media texts are produced within a business or industrial context, and financial structures are designed to produce a positive response from audiences and a profitable return for the product.

In a public service context such as the BBC, financial returns are important but emphasis is also placed on customer satisfaction and ratings to justify taxpayer support through the licence fee.

The control and standardisation of media products by dominant worldwide media organisations, using Western or American value systems, leads to claims of **cultural imperialism**. Concern over the power of these institutions in a globalised economy is a major issue in the study of the media.

Examples of media institutions

- News Corporation
- BBC
- AOL Time-Warner
- MTV
- Disney Corporation
- Vivendi Universal
- Emap
- Sony

TERMINOLOGY

Cultural imperialism: the dominance of Western (particularly American) cultural values across the world as disseminated by the media. For example, American soap operas depicting the American way of life are dubbed into most of the world's important languages and have a worldwide audience. This has the effect of encouraging Western values, aspirations, role models, lifestyles and the consumption of associated consumer goods.

Media ownership

As media technologies develop, so the corporate structure of media industries undergoes constant change and realignment. The coming together of media institutions, or the merger of formerly different elements within one institution, is called **convergence**. The term **synergy** is often used to describe the strengthening outcome of this merging. For example, the parallel releases of a new film with a DVD of the film uses two technologies to maximise a company's revenue from a product.

In the production of news, convergence may mean the development of multimedia newsrooms where print, television, radio and online news are combined through a central news hub, with reporters involved in the generation of news for all media.

Cross-media ownership

Cross-media ownership is a natural commercial consequence of the coming together of the mass media industries in a highly competitive digital age. One outcome is the concentration of ownership increasingly in the hands of a relatively few powerful international corporations and institutions. This involves a media corporation having interest in a range of different media. For example, the News Corporation owns companies involved in newspaper and magazine publishing, book publishing, film making, cable and DBS (satellite) television stations, and radio stations on a global scale.

In Britain, concerns over the tendency towards oligopoly power (where a few large companies dominate the market) have been balanced against the government's wishes: to encourage powerful industrial groupings capable of competing in world markets and to reduce regulation that is seen as inhibiting the natural evolution of media industries.

The issue of whether international conglomerates such as the News Corporation should be allowed to own UK terrestrial television channels is controversial. Channel Five has already given the corporation a foothold by awarding the news contract to Sky rather than, as before, to ITN.

EXAMINER'S TIP

It is important to recognise the commercial nature of all media products. Most of them are constructed by groups of individuals working within organisations that seek a large financial return on the product. This will influence the nature and content of the product, the medium chosen, the pattern of distribution and the target audience.

Point for discussion

The tendency towards convergence in media industries and the commercial and technological pressures towards cross-media ownership tend to favour international conglomerates, with the government in the UK increasingly seeing its regulatory role more in terms of media content than restricting corporate ownership. In 2006, the government restated its commitment to the public service ethos of the BBC, emphasising that it should balance its worldwide commercial activities with its core business of informing, instructing and entertaining the British audience. Issues of quality and type of programme were left deliberately vague.

1.6 Language

Language is a code through which meaning can be expressed and shared by groups of people. In media terms, it describes the sign systems, structures and codes used by a particular medium, such as photographic language, film/moving image language or print medium language.

In written form, language is the basis for recording, passing on and sharing the collective experience of mankind. Pictorial language (such as cave painting) has been the means of expressing core cultural and spiritual values since the earliest times.

- In media studies, language is the code used within a particular medium to convey messages to the audience. Unless the audience can decode messages and share the meanings intended, communication cannot take place.
- These codes are culturally determined and can be culturally specific. This means that they may be understood by some audiences and not by others.

- Media language can be written, verbal, non-verbal and visual.
- The language of film refers to all the elements that make up the construction of a film: sets, lighting, mise-en-scène and editing. In order to read a film, audiences must be familiar with all these elements.

2 Applying the key concepts to text analysis

The key concepts are applied to media texts as part of a **deconstruction** process, where deconstruction is the separation of a text into its component parts and the analysis of these parts. All media texts are **constructed**, usually by working groups or individuals who select and combine their various elements; deconstruction is a reversal of this process. The AQA specification is quite specific in its checklisting of the key concepts, whereas for OCR and WJEC the approach is more implicit but no less important.

2.1 Questions to be considered (AS/A2)

When you analyse a media text using the key concepts, you need to ask yourself a series of questions concerning each concept. Answering these questions will help you to focus your analysis and ensure that you cover all of the important elements.

Genre

- What is the genre, sub-genre or type of media product? For example, is it a magazine advertisement, a television commercial, a television sitcom or a slasher horror movie?
- What are the key **iconographic** elements that identify the genre? In the vampire horror genre these would include vampire teeth, Gothic settings, graveyards, bats, crucifixes, garlic, wooden stakes and coffins.
- What are the **narrative** conventions of the genre? Examples include: 'they all lived happily ever after' in a fairytale; the girl unmasking the killer in a teen slasher horror movie; the storyline being resolved so that everything is back in place for the next episode in a sitcom; and the identification of the product with a positive and desirable lifestyle in an advertisement.
- How does the genre meet or challenge the expectations of an audience? Is the outcome predictable or does it have a twist? Can the audience guess the ending or are they surprised?

The crime thriller *The Usual Suspects* (Bryan Singer 1995) seems to be following a fairly predictable pattern during the prolonged police interview with key witness Verbal Kint (played by Kevin Spacey) concerning the identity of the mysterious gangster Keyser Söze. The police interviewer and the audience are stunned by the sudden realisation in the last moments of the film, as the witness drives away, that he is the elusive gangster. This narrative device has the effect of encouraging the audience to want to see the whole film again, in order to pick up the detail that they missed that gives away the gangster's identity.

TERMINOLOGY

Iconography: the distinguishing elements, in terms of props and visual details, that characterise a genre.

Narrative: the storyline and structure of a media text, which provide a framework of expectation, predictability and outcome.

Remember that a media product does not have to fit into a prescribed genre and that contemporary texts often show characteristics of several genres deigned to appeal to different audiences.

Representation

- Consider who or what is being represented. If it is people, are they men, women or children? What are their race, origin, social class, status, nationality, age and state of health?
- Who (organisations or individuals) is responsible for constructing the representations? Examples are a BBC news team, a charity such as the NSPCC or a pressure group like War on Want.
- What places are represented?
- Are the representations **positive** or **negative**?
- Do the representations involve idealised versions of people and places? Such idealised images include cover girls on teenage magazines such as *Bliss* and *Sugar*, or photographs of Greek islands in a holiday brochure.
- What attitudes, beliefs and values are represented?
- Do the representations confirm or challenge existing stereotypes? For example, in light of the history of slavery, is it possible to represent black people as servants or low-paid agricultural workers without the associated negative connotations?

Positive representation: the representation of a person, place or social group in a way that would generate a positive and favourable response from a viewer, reader or listener, in line with the way in which the person, place or group being represented would wish to be seen and which enhances their sense of value and self-worth.

Negative representation: the representation of a person, place or social group in a way that would create a negative, unfavourable or hostile response from the viewer, reader or listener. This is often in line with prejudiced or stereotyped opinions and views.

Audience

- What is the intended audience for the media product? For example, is it aimed at pre-school children, school children, pre-teens, teenagers, young singles aged 18–30, married couples with or without children, separated singles, middle-aged couples with adult children, retired couples or pensioners? It could be combinations of these.
- How is the audience defined and targeted by the product? Is it a mass audience or a niche audience?
- What is its gender, ethnicity and social class?
- What are the expected preferred readings for the product?
- How does the product reach the audience, and through what media?

Values and ideology

What assumptions does the product make about the **attitudes**, **beliefs** and **values** of the audience, and how are these embedded in the product? Issues you could consider include:

- How does the text represent relations between men and women?
- Is heterosexuality seen as the norm?

- Does the text show violent solutions to disagreements as the norm?
- Does the text assume that people live in nuclear families (a man, a woman and their children)?
- How are older people represented? Are they treated with respect or ridicule?
- Are acquiring and spending money respresented as the principal goals of life
- Which cultures and ethnicities are represented?
- Who and what are not represented?
- Are the values **mainstream** or **alternative**?

Attitudes, beliefs and values: these are terms commonly used when discussing the audience for media products and the factors influencing the reception of media messages.

- **Attitudes:** the positions people adopt in relation to a particular issue, for example being for or against fox hunting.
- **Beliefs:** deeply held views, such as a belief in human equality or a belief in God.
- **Values:** the moral or ideological structures within which beliefs and attitudes are formed, such as a belief in Christianity or Islam.

Mainstream: the uncontroversial, generally accepted attitudes, beliefs and values of the majority population. Mainstream values are influenced by dominant ideology.

Alternative: challenging or opposing the mainstream values of a society in a way that can be controversial and provocative.

Preferred reading: the reading or meaning of a media text intended by its producers.

Negotiated reading: a reading of a text whereby the audience interprets the meaning in the light of its own experience.

Oppositional reading: a reading of a text whereby the audience adopts a position of challenge, rejection and opposition with regard to the intended meaning.

Dominant ideology: the ideology of the ruling elite in a society, accepted by the majority as common sense and reproduced in mainstream media texts.

Point for discussion

Theories of ideology owe much to the work of Antonio Gramsci, the Italian Communist party leader imprisoned by Mussolini. Gramsci used the term 'hegemony' to describe the way in which dominant elites can maintain power over the economic, political and cultural direction of a society. The values that sustain elites in power are reproduced every day by the media and are made to seem like the common sense views of the majority so that any challenge to them is marginalised.

Institutions

- Which business or corporate structures are involved in the production of the media product?
- Under what circumstances is it produced?
- Is it produced by mainstream industry or independently?
- How is the product financed?
- Who profits financially from its creation?
- How is it distributed?
- Under what circumstances is it accessed by the audience? Examples include cinema, home video, computer game, magazine, terrestrial television and satellite television.

Language

- What media languages are involved in the product? Are they written, verbal, non-verbal, aural, visual or a combination of these?
- If the text is a film, how is the language of film used? If verbal or written language is involved, what kind of language is it — formal, colloquial or slang? What is the language **register**? Is there a regional accent? Are other techniques used, such as rhyme or alliteration? Are there any examples of **intertextuality**?

Although media languages may involve the use of the written word and verbal communication, it is important to remember that the term 'language' does not apply exclusively to the written word and verbal communication when used in a media context.

Register: the style and tone of language used in printed and oral/aural media texts. Register includes grammatical features, the choice of vocabulary and the mode of address used, and may involve the use of specialist vocabularies such as legal jargon or the technical terminology used for the specification and performance of cars.

Intertextuality: the practice of deliberately including references to one text in the narrative of another, usually as a device intended to engage the interest of the audience by appealing to their prior knowledge and experience of media texts. For example, in Robert Zemeckis's film *What Lies Beneath* (2000) there are many references to Alfred Hitchcock's *Psycho* (1960), including bathroom scenes (the shower scene in *Psycho*) a menacing ghostly house, a character called Norman (Norman Bates in *Psycho*) a car going under water, a sliver of broken glass resembling the knife used in *Psycho* and, for good measure, there are references to Hitchcock's *Rear Window*, with the partial observation of activity in the neighbours' house through different windows. Finally, the shots using digital technology enhance Hitchcock's camera style, particularly in the shot zooming from a height into the moving car on the bridge, towards the end of the film.

When you begin the assessment of a media text, it is useful to sit back and ask yourself the following:

- What kind of text is it?
- Why was that particular medium chosen?
- How does the choice of medium determine the content of the text?
- Who produced it?
- What is the effect of the text on the audience?
- What is the producer's intention?
- Does it seek to inform, instruct, persuade or entertain, or a combination of these elements?

3 *Wider contexts and the analysis of media texts (A2)*

A distinguishing feature between the work at AS and A2 is the emphasis at A2 on the wider contexts in which media texts are produced. These contexts are described as being: **social**, **historical**, **economic** or **political**, with the acronym **SHEP**. You are

expected to make reference to these in your discussion of media texts. In the outlines below there is inevitably some overlap between the categories. These contexts apply to all A2 units.

3.1 Social contexts

Chronology

Early twentieth century

The social contexts surrounding the creation of media texts involve the prevailing attitudes, beliefs and values at the time a text is produced. This is often called the **Zeitgeist**, a German word meaning 'the spirit of the age'. For example, after the First World War ended in 1918, Germany, as the defeated nation, was in social turmoil, with a fear of communist revolution. However, it also had a liberated and creative arts scene. German cinema produced *Nosferatu* (director F.W. Murnau 1922), with its fears of aliens, disease and plague bringing the collapse of ordered society. The film reflected uncertainties and concerns in Germany, particularly fears of foreign influence reflected in the growth of anti-Semitism. Fear of plague introduced by the alien vampire perhaps related to the flu pandemic of 1918 that killed millions of people in Europe. At the same time, the film illustrated the creative and innovative atmosphere in the arts, with its Expressionist style and innovative use of the camera.

1930s

These were the years of the great economic Depression and growing uncertainty about political developments in Europe. In 1920 the 18th Amendment to the US Constitution had prohibited the manufacture and sale of alcoholic drink. The resulting black market in alcohol gave rise to a huge increase in gangsters and organised crime. Prohibition was abolished in 1933.

Cinema (dominated by Hollywood, the studio system and the great stars) reflected this background, with the development of the gangster movie, such as *Public Enemy* (William Wellman 1931), *Little Caesar* (Mervyn LeRoy 1930) and Howard Hawk's *Scarface* (1932). Hollywood also provided escapist entertainment with films like *The Scarlet Empress* (Joseph Von Sternberg 1934), starring Marlene Dietrich, and the Hollywood musical *Top Hat* (1935), starring Fred Astaire and Ginger Rogers.

1940s and the war years

In Britain, films reflected the need to raise national morale in the face of the threat of invasion; they emphasised self-sacrifice and the need for personal courage in facing the demanding and difficult tasks ahead. In a similar way, cinema in the USA in the 1940s reflected a growing patriotism but also the dark, uncertain and amoral world of wartime in what the French came to call **film noir**, when the films were first shown in France after the liberation of Europe at the end of the war. An example is *Double Indemnity* (Billy Wilder 1944).

1950s and the post-war years

Science fiction films in the 1950s reflected the growing fear of science gone wrong, the horrific consequences of exposure to radiation and fears of mutation with the development of the atom bomb. Examples include *The Blob* (Irvin S. Yeaworth Jr. 1958) and *Creature from the Black Lagoon* (Jack Arnold and John Sherwood 1954). Fear of communism and growing paranoia concerning 'brainwashing' and aliens were reflected in *It Came From Outer Space* (Jack Arnold 1953) and even *Teenagers from Outer Space* (Tom Graeff 1959), in which thrill-crazed space kids blast the flesh off humans.

In Britain, post-war triumphalism led to a whole range of films celebrating wartime achievements, including *The Dam Busters* (Michael Anderson 1955) and *Above Us the Waves* (Ralph Thomas 1955). The Ealing Comedies poked fun at traditional values and social relationships, while the *Carry On* film series (starting with *Carry on Sergeant* (Gerald Thomas 1958)), with its constant sexual innuendo and farcical plots, echoed the slowly changing moral values of the times. Hammer Horror films provided escapist entertainment in the form of highly sexualised vampires at a time when representations of sexual behaviour on screen were heavily censored.

1960s to the present day

From the 1960s, changes in attitudes towards sex, marriage and family life were reflected in the increasingly relaxed censorship of films and written texts, and the increase in violent crime was reflected in more graphic representations of violence in films. Examples include *The Graduate* — sex and controversial relationships (Mike Nichols 1967), *Bonnie and Clyde* — extreme violence with gangsters as antiheroes (Arthur Penn 1967) and *Straw Dogs* — sex and extreme violence (Sam Peckinpah 1971).

The continuing **Cold War** gave rise to a generation of spy thrillers and also spawned the series of James Bond movies based on Ian Fleming's novels — for example, *From Russia with Love* (Terence Young 1963).

Horror and suspense films during this period began to reflect the growing interest in psychology, schizophrenia and the killer as a boy next door rather than a monster or vampire figure (*Psycho*, Alfred Hitchcock 1960; *Halloween*, John Carpenter 1978).

The Vietnam War (1964–1975) provided material for exploration of the horrors of war and its dehumanising effects. Examples include *The Deer Hunter* (Michael Cimino 1978), *Apocalypse Now* (Francis Ford Coppola 1979), *Platoon* (Oliver Stone 1986) and *Full Metal Jacket* (Stanley Kubrick 1987). Science fiction movies ranged from fears of the undead (*Dawn of the Dead*, George Romero 1978) to fears of aliens in space (*Alien*, Ridley Scott 1979) and cosmic disaster (*Armageddon*, Michael Bay 1998). The uncertain future facing the post-Cold-War world, with concerns over terrorism disorder and civil war, provided material for *Blackhawk Down* (Ridley Scott 2001), based on events in Somalia, while the terrorist events of 9/11 were recreated in *World Trade Center* (Oliver Stone 2006) and *Flight 93* (Paul Greengrass 2006).

TERMINOLOGY

Cold War: the military and political standoff that existed between the West, led by the USA, and the communist bloc, led by the Soviet Union, which developed after the end of the Second World War and lasted, with occasional 'thaws', until the collapse of the Soviet Union in 1990. It was 'cold' rather than hot because, although the brink was reached on several occasions — notably the Cuban missile crisis of 1962 — armed conflict between the two superpowers never occurred. Rather than fight each other, the two blocs fought proxy wars by backing one side or the other in local conflicts, notably in the Korean war (1950–53), the war in Congo (1960–64), the Arab–Israeli conflict (1949, 1956, 1967 to the present day), the Vietnam war (1964–1975) and Afghanistan (1980s).

Key media texts

Below are some key media texts that reflect controversial changes in social attitudes from this period.

Lady Chatterley's Lover (D. H. Lawrence 1960). Although originally published in 1930, it was not until 1960 that the uncensored version was published by Penguin. The novel was at the centre of an unsuccessful Crown prosecution for obscenity, and its failure gave rise to the publication of many previously 'banned' texts. The novel contains explicit sex scenes and four letter words.

Psycho (Alfred Hitchcock 1960). This film, regarded as the first 'slasher horror' where the killer is 'the boy next door', was also famous for a discreetly filmed nude shower scene. Several scenes from the film were in fact censored.

Bonnie and Clyde (Arthur Penn 1967). This was the first film after the abolition of the American Hayes Code on censorship to show graphic violence, with bodies shown being hit by bullets.

A Clockwork Orange (Stanley Kubrick 1971). This film was withdrawn from circulation in the UK by the director following many complaints that its portrayal of graphic violence and rape encouraged 'copycat behaviour'. The film reflected growing concern about teenage gang violence.

Last Tango in Paris (Bernardo Bertolucci 1972). This film contains explicit sex scenes in a casual and transient relationship. Although nowhere near as explicit as contemporary films such as *Nine Songs* (Michael Winterbottom 2005), it was subject to a prosecution for obscenity brought by Mary Whitehouse, and banned from many UK cinemas.

The Exorcist (William Friedkin 1973). This famous film about the exorcism of a possessed child contains obscenities, blasphemy and sexual assault with a crucifix, together with exorcism scenes that were shocking to audiences at the time. This combination of sexual swearing, violence and obscenity with the questioning of religious belief was too much for critics like Mary Whitehouse and the Festival of Light. The film was branded as satanic by the evangelist Billy Graham, and it was banned on video release in the UK for 15 years.

Halloween (John Carpenter 1978). This classic suspense slasher horror movie has been imitated and parodied by many since, but perhaps not equalled. It firmly established the generic and narrative conventions of the genre, in particular that sexual promiscuity leads to a violent end and that the 'final girl' (Jamie Lee Curtis as Lauri Strode), who fights back against the killer, is saved. Both these elements had in fact been present in *Psycho*, 18 years earlier.

Alien (Ridley Scott 1979). This was the first space horror movie, with Sigourney Weaver playing one of the first female action heroes, Ellen Ripley. She emerges as the sole survivor of the crew battling an alien monster. The film's most famous scene is the alien offspring exploding from crewman Kane's stomach, in a grotesque parody of a male giving birth.

Nightmare on Elm Street (Wes Craven 1984). A teen slasher horror classic.

Thelma and Louise (Ridley Scott 1991). This was a new take on the buddy/road movie. The buddies are women who take to the road after one of them kills a predatory male following the rescue of her friend from an attempted rape. They find freedom by breaking away from violent, stultifying and conventional relationships, but become fugitives pursued by the male forces of authority. The film reflected the growing challenge to orthodox representations of gender, with the women portrayed as victims of male sexual violence, indifference and duplicity. It ends with a car chase in which the

women choose suicide by driving into a canyon (a famous freeze-frame closing shot) rather than submission to the pursuing male police officers.

Natural Born Killers (Oliver Stone 1994). This is a reworking of a classic *folie à deux*, based on the true story of a runaway teenage couple's orgy of violent crime and murder and the celebrity status awarded to them by media coverage. The film was heavily criticised for glorifying violence and encouraging 'copycat' crime, but in fact raised important issues concerning media-generated 'celebrity' culture.

Trainspotting (Jimmie Boyle 1996). This graphic black comedy deals with the realities of heroin addiction. It reflected the more open discussion of drug addiction and its social consequences.

Queer as Folk (Charles McDougall and Sarah Harding 1999). This Channel 4 production deals explicitly with promiscuous gay relationships involving young people. The series portrays frankly and non-judgementally the sexual behaviour of gay men in a way not seen before on British television.

Dirty Pretty Things (Stephen Frears 2002). This is a graphic representation of the plight suffered by asylum seekers and economic migrants, and the exploitation and deprivation they face. The film challenges stereotypical representations of asylum seekers as a threat, suggested in much contemporary media coverage, and shows them rather as vulnerable victims of unscrupulous individuals.

Brokeback Mountain (Ang Lee 2005). This film is a sympathetic and positive represen-tation of homosexual cowboys in a western genre setting. It demonstrates the change in social attitudes towards representations of sexuality, particularly in this most macho of traditional genres.

Nine Songs (Michael Winterbottom 2005). This is the simple story of a love affair between a young American woman and her English boyfriend, narrated by the boyfriend against a background of rock concerts. What makes it so startling is the graphic and explicit representation of their sexual relationship in a way not seen before in British mainstream cinema. The film pushes the boundary of what is acceptable in the multiplex cinema and challenges the distinction between sex as pornography and sex in the mainstream.

Media texts continue to mirror social change, with increasingly positive representations of women and ethnic minority groups and a less homophobic representation of gay relationships; this reflects equal rights and anti-discrimination legislation.

3.2 Historical contexts

The time at which a media text is produced influences the content and ideology of that text. It is important that you have a good general knowledge of key historical events of the twentieth century and beyond.

Chronology

As a means of contextualising political and historical events against some important media and cultural developments, a brief and selective chronology is provided below for easy reference.

1901
- Death of Queen Victoria

1901–14

- Growth of the suffragette movement, which demanded votes for women
- *Titanic* disaster (1912)
- Beginning of modernist movement in architecture and the arts
- Early development of radio
- First moving pictures shown in cinemas

1914–18

- First World War: Germany, Austria-Hungary and Turkey (the Central Powers) at war with Britain, France, Russia and Italy (from 1915), and with the USA from 1917
- Women replace men drafted into the army in many factory and civilian roles
- Great changes in social order, with disruption of domestic life, mass drafting of young men from the countryside and weakening of the traditional class systems
- War in Europe encourages the growth of the Hollywood film industry
- Revolution in Russia (1917) and the rise of Lenin and communism
- Women over 30 granted the vote in Britain (1918)
- Flu epidemic kills 50 million people worldwide

1920

- The 18th amendment to the US Constitution introduces the prohibition of the sale and manufacture of alcohol across the USA

1922

- *Nosferatu* is released — the first vampire film — with the theme of plague
- German Expressionist cinema flourishes
- Benito Mussolini takes power in Italy as leader of an anti-communist Fascist government
- Founding of the BBC

1924

- Stalin replaces Lenin as Communist Russian leader
- The first Labour government in Britain assumes power

1926

- The trade union movement calls a general strike in Britain

1927

- First talking picture, *The Jazz Singer* (Alan Crosland), is released
- Prohibition era in the USA, and a growth of gangster violence

1928

- All women over 21 granted the vote in Britain, giving women voting equality with men

1929

- Wall Street crash — the stock market hits bottom and millions of people ruined; start of the great economic Depression

1930

- Golden age of Hollywood studios begins (1930–48)

1931

- First vampire 'talkie' released: Tod Browning's *Dracula,* with Bela Lugosi

1933

- Adolf Hitler and the Nazi party come to power in Germany
- Persecution of the Jews begins in Germany
- Opponents of Stalin inprisoned and executed in Russia during Communist party 'purges'
- Germany and Russia become totalitarian police states, with prison camps and oppressive rule
- Prohibition is ended in the USA

1936

- Spain convulsed by civil war between communists and fascists
- Japan invades Manchuria and China
- Italy invades Ethiopia
- Newly developed 'television' seen in Britain and at the Berlin Olympics in Germany

1937

- First technicolor feature cartoon film, Walt Disney's *Snow White and the Seven Dwarfs*, released

1939

- Outbreak of the Second World War after German invasion of Poland
- US Civil War epic *Gone with the Wind* (Walter Fleming) released

1940

- Germany invades and occupies France, Belgium, Holland, Denmark and Norway; Battle of Britain air combat over the skies of southern England

1941

- Germany invades North Africa, the Balkans, Greece and Russia; Japan attacks the USA and overruns large areas of southeast Asia
- *Citizen Kane* (Orson Welles) produced in the USA

1942/3

- German army heavily defeated by Russians at Stalingrad (now Volgograd)
- Air bombardment of German cities begins
- Nazis begin the extermination of European Jews in concentration camps

1944

- British and American landing in France on D-day
- Emergence of film noir in America, for example Billy Wilder's *Double Indemnity*

1945

- British, American, French and Russian troops overrun and occupy Germany and central Europe, ending the European war
- Atomic bombs developed by American, British and European scientists are dropped on the Japanese cities of Hiroshima and Nagasaki, ending the war with Japan
- Over 50 million people have been killed during the war, including 6 million Jews murdered in concentration camps
- The war leaves the USA and Soviet Russia as the dominant world powers
- During the war, women had replaced men in factory and civilian roles and played military roles in all countries; in Russia, women were directly involved as combatants in the air and on land

- Labour government elected in Britain, leading to the creation of the welfare state and the founding of the National Health Service

1946

- United Nations Organization founded, with headquarters in New York
- Russians draw 'Iron Curtain' across divided Germany and the part of Europe it occupies
- Austerity and food rationing continue in a Britain still exhausted and impoverished by the cost of the war

1947

- Russian attempts to isolate Berlin lead to the Berlin air lift dispute with the Western powers and the beginning of the Cold War
- Disastrous fuel shortages in Britain during severe winter

1948

- George Orwell writes *1984*, predicting a grim, totalitarian police state future dominated by the 'telescreen'
- State of Israel founded in Palestine; Arab nations resist by force and Palestinian Arabs become refugees; start of the Arab–Israeli conflict

1949

- Foundation of NATO to resist possible Russian advances in Europe
- Communist revolution in China under Mao Tse Tung (Mao Zedong)
- Britain leaves India and Burma and fights guerrilla war in Malaya; end of the British Empire in the Far East
- State of Pakistan created by British partition of India
- Growth of television ownership in the USA

1950–52

- Korean War, involving British, American and United Nations troops in fighting Korean communist and Chinese forces
- Fears of communist conspiracy leads to McCarthy witch hunt era in the USA
- Newly elected Conservative government in Britain promises an end to austerity and heralds a period of growing affluence

1953

- Death of Stalin
- Threat of nuclear war grows as H-bombs are tested by Russia and America
- Coronation of Elizabeth II
- Growth of television and car ownership in Britain
- Growth of teenage culture; in Britain, the growth of rock and roll sees the emergence of 'teddy boys' wearing drainpipe trousers, Edwardian style jackets, brothel creeper shoes and greased, swept back hair; gang violence causes press controversy
- Marlon Brando stars in *The Wild One* (Laslo Benedek)

1955

- Founding of ITV ends BBC broadcasting monopoly
- *Rebel Without a Cause* (Nicolas Ray) is released, starring James Dean

1956

- British and French forces invade Egypt over the Suez crisis but are forced to withdraw through lack of US support

- Foundation of the European Common Market by the Treaty of Rome
- New Russian leader Khrushchev denounces the genocidal policies of Stalin
- Russian tanks crush uprising in Hungary

1959

- Harold Macmillan, the British Prime Minister, makes a speech about the end of colonialism and the 'wind of change' blowing in Africa; in the same year, Britain begins colonial withdrawal that signals the end of the British Empire in Africa
- Civil rights movement founded in the USA, demanding equality for black people
- British 'kitchen sink' cinema popular, with *Look Back in Anger* (Tony Richardson 1958) and *Room at the Top* (Jack Clayton 1959)
- Macmillan tells the British that the new consumer society and greater prosperity mean 'you've never had it so good'
- Television ownership now commonplace in Britain

1960

- Russian cosmonaut Yuri Gagarin is the first man in space, marking the beginning of the space race between the USA and USSR
- Obscenity trial of Penguin books for the publication of D. H. Lawrence's *Lady Chatterley's Lover* takes place; Penguin wins the case on an 'artistic merit' defence, leading to a relaxation of censorship of the written word
- Apartheid policy of racial separation leads to the UN's isolation of white-dominated South Africa
- British New Wave cinema: *Saturday Night and Sunday Morning* (Karel Reisz), a realist film of Alan Sillitoe's novel exploring working class sexual relationships; later followed by *A Taste of Honey* (Tony Richardson 1961) and *A Kind of Loving* (John Schlesinger 1962)

1961

- Contraceptive pill introduced, giving women greater control of their sexual behaviour

1962

- Cuban missile crisis brings the greatest threat of nuclear war between Russia and US and Western powers
- Huge military arsenals and world dominance leads to the USA and Russia being designated 'Superpowers'
- BBC2 begins transmission

1963

- US President John F. Kennedy assassinated in Dallas, Texas
- 'Beatlemania' sweeps Britain and the US as fans express their devotion to the Liverpool band
- Era of the miniskirt and an increased frankness about sex
- The 'Profumo Affair' — a sex and spy scandal that rocks the Conservative government

1964

- Beginning of serious US military involvement in the Vietnam War
- Civil Rights Act passed by President Lyndon Johnson grants equality to black US citizens
- Labour government elected under Harold Wilson
- Mods and rockers fight in English seaside resorts
- The Beatles feature in the film *A Hard Day's Night* (Richard Lester)

1966
- Harold Wilson wins landslide victory for Labour in election
- The swinging sixties, flower power and the rock music revolution grip youth culture

1967
- Homosexuality and abortion decriminalised in Britain
- War between Israel and Arab state leads to Israel's occupation of the West Bank and Gaza territories
- Colour television introduced in Britain
- LSD psychedelic revolution
- The Beatles' *Sergeant Pepper* album released
- Home Secretary Roy Jenkins coins the term 'permissive society'
- Dustin Hoffman stars in *The Graduate* (Mike Nichols)

1968
- Assassination of Martin Luther King and Robert F. Kennedy
- Russian tanks suppress liberal movement in Czechoslovakia
- Student riots in Paris against General de Gaulle's government
- USA suffers major military reversal in North Vietnamese 'Tet Offensive'
- Large and violent anti-Vietnam War demonstration at the American Embassy in London, as worldwide criticism of US involvement grows
- Richard Nixon wins US presidential election

1969
- USA lands the first man on the moon

1970
- Publication of *The Female Eunuch* by Germaine Greer
- Growth of feminism and demands for gender equality
- Conservatives unexpectedly win general election

1973
- Oil crisis leads to three-day working week in Britain
- Miners' strike threatens Conservative government
- Britain under Edward Heath joins the European Community
- Films *Last Tango in Paris* (Bernardo Bertolucci 1972) and *The Exorcist* (William Friedkin 1973) cause controversy in the UK
- 'Festival of Light' pressure group campaigns against pornography and violence in film
- 'Teenybopper culture' begins: fascination with such stars as David Cassidy, the Bay City Rollers, the Jackson Five and the Osmonds

1974
- Watergate scandal forces resignation of US President Richard Nixon
- Labour wins general election

1975
- USA withdraws from Vietnam, ending the war

1976
- Punk revolution with the *Sex Pistols*
- Harold Wilson resigns as Prime Minister and James Callaghan takes over

1977

- Death of Elvis Presley

1979–80

- 'Winter of discontent' in Britain caused by strikes in public services
- Margaret Thatcher comes to power
- Fall of the Shah of Iran in an Islamic revolution led by Ayatollah Khomeini
- American Embassy hostages taken by Islamic revolutionaries in Iran
- Russians invade Afghanistan to support communist government
- John Lennon shot dead in New York

1981

- Economic depression; unemployment reaches 3 million as government experiments with 'monetarist economics'
- New Romantics emerged as a glamorous backlash against punk rock, with bands such as Adam and the Ants, Spandau Ballet and Duran Duran

1982

- Falklands War against Argentina
- USA supports Islamic fundamentalist rebels led by Osama Bin Laden fighting Russians in Afghanistan
- AIDS identified and named

1983

- Margaret Thatcher wins second term with an agenda of 'there is no alternative'
- First high-profile media coverage of AIDS

1984

- Miners' strike; defeat of the trade unions by Thatcher government
- Privatisation and free market economics determine government policy
- Channel 4 begins transmission

1986

- Widespread homophobic reaction to AIDS

1989–90

- Collapse of communism in Russia and Eastern Europe
- Fall of the Berlin wall — Germany reunited after 45 years
- Post-communist 'globalisation' of world economic system begins
- 'Madchester' rave music scene — house music and Ecstasy

1991

- John Major succeeds Thatcher
- First Gulf War, following Saddam Hussein's invasion of Kuwait
- Development of the internet

1994–95

- End of apartheid in South Africa with the election of Nelson Mandela
- Film *Natural Born Killers* (Oliver Stone 1995) causes controversy

1997

- New Labour wins power under Tony Blair after 17 years of Conservative government

- Kyoto Agreement signed by states, attempting to limit global warming and environmental damage by reducing carbon dioxide emissions; the biggest polluter (the USA) refuses to sign
- Mobile phone ownership growing fast

2000

- George W. Bush proclaimed US president by a Supreme Court ruling after the most contested US presidential election in history and claims of vote rigging
- Project for New American Century sees the USA as globally dominant

2001

- Terrorist attack on the World Trade Center towers in New York — '9/11'; over 3000 people killed; President Bush declares a 'war on terror'
- Growth of Palestinian suicide bombings in continuing conflict with Israel

2002

- USA leads invasion of Afghanistan to suppress the Taliban fundamentalists, with UN and European support
- *Bowling for Columbine*, Michael Moore's critique of American gun culture, is released
- Growth of celebrity culture and reality television (*Big Brother*)

2003

- US and British forces invade Iraq in search of 'weapons of mass destruction' and to depose dictator Sadam Hussein

2004

- Growth of Chinese, Indian and South American economies
- Fears of growth in number of states owning nuclear weapons as North Korea demands the right to the technology; the USA, Britain, France, Russia, China, India, Pakistan and Israel have large nuclear arsenals
- Growth of digital television

2005

- Fundamentalist government takes power in Iran and demands the right to develop nuclear weapons technology
- Increasing evidence that global warming is leading to climate change
- Continuing insurgency in Iraq
- Islamic terrorist bombs in London: '7/7'
- Enlargement of the European Union to include Poland and other former East European communist states

2006

- Continuing war in Afghanistan against revived Taliban Islamic fundamentalists operating from inside Pakistan
- Terrorist alert in London in September, following the foiling of a plot to bomb airline flights to America.
- Continuing concern over the rise in clandestine immigration to the US and Europe from third-world countries.
- Israel invades southern Lebanon and bombs Gaza in response to terrorist attacks
- North Korea defies the UN and tests a nuclear bomb in October.

It is important to be able to see media texts in their historical context and not to judge them by today's standards and values. For example, the portrayal of black people in *Gone with the Wind* (Walter Fleming 1939) is often cited as being racist and is unacceptable by today's standards. However, when the film is seen in context as a 1930s attempt to portray the values of the 1860s, the representation of black characters is in keeping with the way some Southern families treated their servants. The dominant ideology — that slavery was wrong and that the South deserved to lose the Civil War — provides the background for sympathetic portrayal of strong emotions, human tragedy, personal courage and the pressures on individual families and relationships.

3.3 Economic contexts

The principal economic contexts determining the nature of media texts are the commercial and financial structures within which they are produced — the companies and organisations that generate and finance media products. In the contemporary world, it is usually international corporations that dominate media production and distribution.

How do these contexts influence media texts?

Economic contexts run parallel to historical and social developments (partly outlined above). Major developments and changes over the period are reflected in media texts in terms of content, distribution and production values. Such developments include:

- the First World War in Europe (1914–18), which encouraged the expansion of the US film industry as directors and stars moved away from the conflict
- the Depression of the 1930s
- the war economy in the 1940s, which saw the increasing importance of women in the workforce
- post-war economic austerity in Britain but growing affluence in the USA
- British consumer growth in the 1950s, continuing in the 1960s with increased consumer spending power and the growing economic independence of women
- the oil crisis in the 1970s and the beginning of an economic recession
- equal rights and equal pay for women workers during the 1970s
- economic recession in the 1980s and the slow de-industrialisation of western nations
- growth of a new consumer boom in the late 1980s and into the 1990s, with the service industry/lifestyle economy and the established economic power of women in western societies
- globalisation since 2000, with a dramatic growth of Chinese, South American and Indian economies; fears of a world energy shortage and the economic effects of climate change; continuing large-scale economic migration from developing countries to the developed world; manufacturing industries increasingly transferred from western states to developing economies

Economic contexts and the development of media technologies

The economic conditions of production are important in terms of the development of media technologies, as technological possibility needs to combine with product availability at prices that consumers can afford. The best conditions are a combination of affluent consumers with keenly priced and available products.

- In the 1930s, studios provided escapist cinema entertainment and big stars to draw people away from the stark economic realities. Cinema attendance was cheap and affordable to all.
- Wartime austerity was reflected in low-budget, morale-boosting movies. Radio remained the principal medium of communication, its status enhanced in Britain by its wartime role as the voice of the nation.
- Television, invented in the 1930s but held back by the Second World War, only became available to all in Britain at prices people could afford in the mid-1950s. Cathode ray screen technology used in televisions was developed during the war for military purposes.
- Television ownership resulted in declining cinema audiences and the closure of many cinemas in the 1950s and 1960s. Studios met television competition with epic colour productions in cinemascope that black and white television of the time could not match, such as *The Ten Commandments* (Cecil B. DeMille 1956 and *Cleopatra* (Joseph Mankiewicz 1963).
- Since the 1980s, the production and distribution of films has undergone a transformation in line with the development of video, DVD and internet technologies, with multiplex cinemas now forming only one of several outlets and sources of profit.
- The development of IT — leading to the wide availability of mobile phones and universal access to the internet during the 1990s — has transformed the contexts of media consumption. CGIs (computer generated images) dominate big budget film production.
- The further development of digital systems is anticipated during the coming decade and traditional television reception based on time-sequenced programme schedules will give way to a consumer-based multi-channel service, where viewers can choose any programme at will and watch on combined television/computer screens or even mobile phones.
- Access to television programmes via broadband internet provides new challenges.

3.4 Political contexts

Political contexts affect how media texts are produced, and political values are reflected in these texts. Repressive communist, fascist, militarist and theocratic regimes control and censor content and use the media for propaganda and to maintain enforced values and beliefs. At the time of writing, the media are restricted and subject to government interference in China, Burma, Syria, Iran, Egypt and some other Arab states, former Soviet republics such as Belarus, Zimbabwe and some other African states.

Film and political propaganda
- In the early years of Soviet Russia, the films of Sergei Eisenstein, such as *Battleship Potemkin* (1926) and *October (Ten Days that Shook the World)* (1928), were used to carry the revolutionary message.
- Eisenstein's *Alexander Nevsky* (1938) was used as propaganda to boost Russian morale in the face of the 1941 German invasion.
- The antiwar film *All Quiet on the Western Front* (Lewis Milestone 1930) was so successful in exposing the inhuman futility of war that it was banned in Nazi Germany.
- Leni Riefenstahl's film of a Nuremburg Nazi party rally, *Triumph of the Will* (1936), is one of the first and finest examples of how film can successfully be used as political propaganda.

- In the 1940s, British wartime cinema productions were extensively used in support of wartime propaganda, an example being *In Which we Serve* (David Lean 1942).
- More recent films like *Green Berets* (John Wayne 1968) were used to convey a patriotic view of the unpopular Vietnam War.
- Although not overtly propagandist, Francis Ford Coppola's account of the Vietnam war *Apocalypse Now* (1979) provides a devastating indictment of the war and its dehumanising consequences.
- Steven Spielberg's film *Schindler's List* (1993) brought the horrific realities of the Jewish Holocaust to a new generation and was a powerful reminder of the consequences of political extremism and racist attitudes.
- *Blackhawk Down* (Ridley Scott 2001) has been used to rally US public opinion in support of the Iraq invasion and the so called 'war on terror'.

Political and social messages in film from the 1960s
- British films of the 1960s 'new wave' carried social and political messages. Examples include Lindsay Anderson's *This Sporting Life* (1963) and *If* (1968).
- British social realist director Ken Loach mixes social and political comment in his films — for example, *Sweet Sixteen* (2002).
- *Easy Rider* (Dennis Hopper and Peter Fonda 1969) provided a social commentary on aspects of the hippy culture in the USA and its conflict with traditional values.
- Films like *Brassed Off* (Mark Herman 1996) combined Ealing Comedy with social bite, and *The Full Monty* (Peter Catanneo 1997) provided human drama against the background of industrial decline and the end of trade union power during the 1980s.
- The French film *La Haine* (Mathieu Kassovitz 1995) offers a keen insight into life in the deprived immigrant suburbs of Paris, with clear political implications regarding immigration policies and discrimination.
- *Dirty Pretty Things* (Stephen Frear 2002) provides a social commentary on the plight of asylum seekers in Britain.
- From the 1980s, increasing concerns about the growth of state or alien power through misuse of technology, the loss of individual freedom and the threat of global environmental catastrophe were reflected in many media texts. Examples include *Bladerunner* (Ridley Scott 1982), *Terminator* (James Cameron 1991), *Aliens* (James Cameron 1986) and *The Matrix* trilogy (Wachowski Brothers 1999).
- In the early 1990s, the collapse of communism led to the breakdown of traditional ideological conflict between East and West, and there was increasing focus on the need to champion universal human rights in a world divided between poverty and affluence (e.g. *The Constant Gardener*, Fernando Meirelles 2005).
- Michael Moore's films *Bowling for Columbine* (2002) and *Farenheit 9/11* (2004) were big screen documentaries with clear political messages that challenged US gun culture and the US presidency's response to the 9/11 attacks.
- The contemporary world is increasingly focused on the divide between Western values and traditional religious values, revived in the Islamic world and emphasised by the continuing conflict between Israel and Palestine in the Middle East (e.g. *Jenin Jenin*, Mohamed Bakri 2002).
- Since 2000, the issues of climate change, globalisation of economies and the environment have increasingly been making an impact on political decision making, and this has been reflected in media products (e.g. *The Day After Tomorrow*, Roland Emmerich 2004). World poverty, population pressure and the largely unreported wars

and conflicts in Africa provide the background to continued economic migration into Europe and the USA from the developing world (*Dirty Pretty Things*, Stephen Frear 2002).

Political correctness

The concept of political correctness developed in the USA in the 1970s and was intended to encourage the support for liberation movements and progressive opinion regarding the equality of representation of minority groups and women.

The term entered common usage during the 1980s and applies to media content and attitudes, beliefs and values in general. It is based on the belief that the use of language that carries negative connotations of particular races or social groups, and the expression of certain beliefs and attitudes, should be discouraged or even made a criminal offence, as it is prejudicial to the social recognition of these groups and their positive advancement.

Critics see the practice as repressive of comment and honest opinion.

Political satire

Political satire involves the ridiculing of politicians, their parties and their policies and is a distinctive media form. Examples include the television series *Bremner, Bird and Fortune* and the magazine *Private Eye*. Satire usually has a serious purpose, as seen in Michael Moore's film *Fahrenheit 9/11* (2004), which combines the ridiculing of the Bush presidency with serious comment on the consequences of US foreign policy.

Political satire and comedy are an important part of a free media, as demonstrated by the controversy and debate over the recent Religious and Racial Hatred Bill (defeated in Parliament in 2006), which was opposed by many actors and journalists as limiting free speech and comment. There was equal controversy aroused by the publication in Denmark of cartoons depicting the prophet Mohammed in early 2006.

The analysis of the moving image or print medium text forms a part of AQA and OCR assessment procedures and involves the viewing of previously unseen material under examination conditions. This chapter outlines what is involved in this process and how you can best prepare yourself to tackle the tasks set.

1 *Specification focus: AQA Unit 1 (AS)*

Unit 1: (Reading the media), allows for moving image or print medium extracts to be offered for analysis; the actual choice is only made known in the weeks leading up to the examination. In either case, the question format is the same, with a requirement to provide a written analysis of the texts, working through the key concepts.

If the choice in your examination series is moving image, it is important to practise your note taking skills in preparation for this unit, as you will have 15 minutes of reading and viewing time during which notes are made.

The key concepts are used as a check list and the examination paper offers further guidance on matters to be addressed. You must then write a continuous assessment of the piece you have viewed, exploring all the key concepts as they apply to the text.

It is important that your assessment is not just a description of the texts presented to you. It must be an analysis, using the key concepts and providing an explanation of why and how the text has been constructed the way it is. Where appropriate, you can make connections with other media texts you are familiar with and explore intertextual features, but your focus should be on the material in front of you.

EXAMINER'S TIP

One method of taking notes is to write the key concepts down and draw spider diagrams around them as you notice key elements. For example, if you are presented with an advertisement for trainers using David Beckham, you might start with genre:

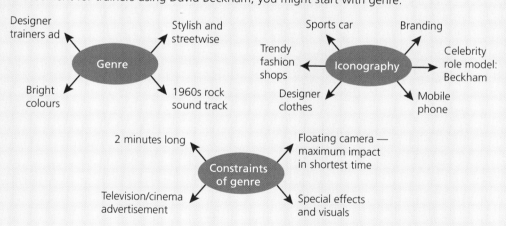

2 *Specification focus: AQA Unit 6 (A2)*

In this A2 module, you will need to demonstrate your critical reading of media texts using the key concepts, and to draw on your wider knowledge of theories, debates and information. You will also be expected to use your knowledge of a range of relevant social, historical, political and economic contextual factors. Visual text analysis is one of the assessment options.

A comparative critical analysis involves applying the key concepts together with the wider social, historical, economic and political contexts. These may be drawn from the same genre but produced under different circumstances, for different audiences and at different times. In making the comparison, you should draw attention to the factors that create similarities and differences in the text and explore the wider contexts and circumstances of production and consumption.

The specification allows for print and/or visual media to be set for study, and you should practise for the unit by reading/viewing and taking notes on a range of texts for comparison. The unit is synoptic and you should draw on all the experience and knowledge gained during your course when evaluating the texts.

EXAMINER'S TIP

Always ask yourself why the examiners chose the materials offered to you. There will be some clear purpose or link between them — obvious issues to compare and contrast. For example, publicity materials for the films *Spartacus* (Stanley Kubrick 1960) and *Gladiator* (Ridley Scott 2000) were used on an AQA paper. The materials provided included posters and VHS video covers, but not clips from the films.

Candidates were given the production dates of both films, thus enabling them to be placed in their contexts. *Spartacus* was produced in 1960 at the height of the Cold War; *Gladiator* dates from 2000, when comparisons were being made between the world dominance of the USA and Ancient Rome.

Both of the films are in the 'sword and sandals' genre, with *Gladiator* embellished with impressive CGIs and a star cast. The films both feature an all-star cast and a famous director. The publicity material made it obvious that the reissued video of *Spartacus* was attempting to benefit from the success of *Gladiator*, to win a new contemporary audience for the classic film.

Representations of male and female leads on the posters showed clearly the change in attitude towards male and female roles in the 40 years separating the productions: the female representation in *Spartacus* was submissive and secondary to Kirk Douglas as the male lead; on the *Gladiator* poster, the female lead, although not dominant, was clearly equal to the male.

The materials provided these and many other obvious points of comparison that you would be expected to make. Remember that the date of production and other details are included in the descriptive brief provided on the paper, and this can be a great help.

Examples of texts for comparison
- *The Italian Job* — comparison of the original (Peter Collinson 1969) with the remake (F. Gary Gray 2003)
- *Open Your Eyes* (Alejandro Amenabar 1997) and *Vanilla Sky* (Cameron Crowe 2001); comparison of scenes
- *Spartacus* (Stanley Kubrick 1960) and *Gladiator* (Ridley Scott 2000); film clips and publicity for both films
- Clips from the television series *The Sweeny* compared with *The Bill*
- *Doctor Who* (1964) compared with *Doctor Who* (2006)
- BBC television news presentations in the 1960s and the present day
- *Cape Fear* — comparison of the original (J. Lee Thompson 1962) with the remake (Martin Scorsese 1991)
- *Take your Pick* (1960s game show) with *The Weakest Link*
- *Double Your Money* with *Who Wants to be a Millionaire?*

- 1960s soap powder advertisements with current ads — print or television/film
- Car advertising in the 1960s and the twenty-first century
- 1950s women's magazines (*Woman's Own, Woman, Woman and Home*) compared with contemporary women's magazines
- *Coronation Street* (1966) compared with *Coronation Street* (2006)

3 Technical aspects of the moving image

Understanding the technical aspects of moving image production and the correct use of terminology is important in assignments and written examinations for all specifications, and in particular OCR AS Unit 2731 (first half).

3.1 Camera angle

Camera angle is the positioning and behaviour of the camera in relation to the subject and is described using the following terminology:

POV: point of view — the camera takes the viewpoint of a character, as with the unseen killer in slasher horror movies such as *Halloween* (John Carpenter 1978).

BCU: 'big close up' — a close-up camera shot showing prominent detail and facial expressions. This is used to create intimacy and audience engagement with the thoughts and emotions of the character.

Long-shot: the camera is a long way from the subject being filmed.

Low angle: the camera is placed below the subject, making the subject seem powerful and dominant.

High angle: the camera looks down on the subject, giving the audience a sense of surveying the scene and dominating the characters and action.

Crane shot: the camera is mounted on a crane, allowing it to swoop down on the subject from a great height.

Dutch angle: the camera is tilted to produce a disorientating effect; this is often used to create the sense of a disordered or disturbed world or individual.

Pan: the camera scans slowly from one side to the other across a wide area; this is often used in establishing shots, such as in the opening scene of *Psycho* (Alfred Hitchcock 1960).

Tilt: the camera scans the scene from top to bottom (or vice versa).

Following shot: the camera follows the subject; this is often used as a POV shot, where one person is following another.

Eye-level shot: the camera is positioned at head height, creating a sense of normal viewing for the audience.

Tracking shot: the camera runs smoothly on tracks alongside the subject.

Dolly shot: in studio shots, the camera is mounted on a dolly — a trolley that allows movement in different directions.

Hand held: the camera takes on the jerky movements of the camera operator as it moves around. This is used with great effect in *The Blair Witch Project* (Daniel Myrick 1999).

Crabbed shot: the camera is placed in a confined space, such as the inside of a cupboard.

Master shot: a camera shot used at the beginning of a sequence to establish the component elements in such a way as to allow the audience to make sense of the action that follows.

Establishing shot: a long shot, the opening shot of a film or a sequence within a film, where the location of the action is established. A long shot panning across a cityscape establishes that the action takes place within the city, as seen in the opening scene of *Psycho* (Alfred Hitchcock 1960).

Steadycam: the camera is strapped to the camera operator with a harness and can move in any direction, creating a smooth floating effect.

3.2 Other film terminology

Gaffer: a member of the film production team who acts as chief technician, particularly with regard to lighting.

Lip synchronisation: the post-production practice of adding dubbed dialogue in such a way as to ensure that it coordinates with the lip movements of the actors.

Grip: an individual on the film set responsible for moving and arranging scenery, lighting, cameras and other equipment.

Film stock: unexposed film yet to be used in production.

3.3 Editing

Editing is the process of assembling the pieces of a media text to produce a completed artefact. The term applies to magazines and newspapers as well as the visual image product. The individual responsible for the compilation of print media products is called the editor. With film, the process is usually completed by the director and is often constrained by commercial values to do with the film's intended audience, marketing and distribution. The commercial version of a film represents only a percentage of the scenes actually shot and it is normal for many scenes to be discarded during the editing process for the following reasons:

- **commercial** — the film may be too long or the narrative too complex
- **aesthetic** — some scenes may be considered unsuccessful during the editing process
- **censorial** — scenes with sexual or violent content may be cut at the request of the British Board of Film Classification, or for commercial or marketing reasons, to ensure acceptability under a chosen classification certificate.

Editor's cut

The editor's cut of a film is his or her version that reflects personal choices and decisions uninfluenced by market pressure; it is often seen as having greater artistic value as opposed to commercial value. Films with an editor's cut include *Bladerunner* (Ridley Scott 1982), *Apocalypse Now* (Francis Ford Coppola 1979) and *Donnie Darko* (Richard Kelly 2001).

Film editing terms

Razor edit: where there is a sharp cut between one scene and another

Fade: where the scene slowly disappears, leaving a black or white screen

Iris fade: where the scene slowly contracts as a circular image

Dissolve: where one scene slowly dissolves into another

Cutaway: where a brief shot of a related action is cut into a scene

Montage: the process of placing once scene after another to create a running narrative

Eye line match: where the character's eye line is maintained when the camera cuts from viewing the character to viewing what the character sees; this creates the effect that what the camera sees is what the character sees

3.4 Sound

Sound can be:

- **digetic** — part of the action, for example words spoken by characters, traffic noise in a street scene or birdsong in a country scene
- **non-digetic** — not part of the action, such as a symphony orchestra playing during a battle scene
- **narrated** — through voice-over

EXAMINER'S TIP

Always try to use the appropriate media terminology when completing a media studies assignment or answering an exam question. Using the right words shows the examiner that you know your subject.

3.5 Special effects/graphics

- **CGIs:** computer-generated images
- **Pyrotechnics:** fires and explosions
- **Stunts:** either real or simulated by CGIs
- **Computer-generated graphics**

3.6 Mise-en-scène

Mise-en-scène comprises the total contents of the framed image, which includes settings, props, décor, lighting, characters, positioning, framing and the total look of the scene.

Point for discussion

The way in which a scene is framed will affect how the viewer reads the importance of all the elements in it, regardless of the fact that the characters and dialogue remain the same. To illustrate the nature and importance of framing, imagine you are holding an empty picture frame in front of a scene to be filmed. Hold it in front of you and take note of the area of the scene it contains; if there are people, look at who is in the foreground and background. Consider which aspects of the scene seem most important. Then move your position and hold up the frame against the same scene but from a different location. How have all the elements changed? Which elements now seem important? Are any excluded?

4 *Semiology and text analysis (AS/A2)*

Semiology (or semiotics) is the study of signs and their meanings, and is an important method of text analysis.

4.1 Terminology and principles

All shared cultural meaning is derived from the construction of signs, which consist of that which is signified (the idea or object) and the signifier (what is used to represent that object, such as a drawing of a tree signifying the real object tree).

The signified and signifier together constitute a sign. The first or simplest level of meaning is that of **denotation** — for example, a photograph of a rose denotes or stands for the rose flower.

The second, more complex, level of meaning is one of **connotation**, where cultural knowledge and values add metaphorical meaning to the sign. An example is a photograph of a red rose, which can signify New Labour, England or, on Valentine's Day, passion. Complex connotations can form cultural **myths**, such as pictures of the English countryside indicating healthy life, clean air, tradition and heritage.

4.2 Classification and characteristics of signs

Signs can be classified by types: indexical signs are where the meaning is implied, for example the Eiffel tower standing for Paris. Signs can also be iconic — where the sign looks like what it refers to, such as a photograph, or symbolic — where there is no obvious relationship, for example the three point star badge standing for Mercedes Benz. Symbolic signs can develop fixed or anchored cultural meanings, which makes it difficult to use them in other contexts.

- Although the swastika is an ancient Greek pattern design and a Hindu sign for the sun, with connotations of good luck and happiness, its use by Hitler as the symbol of Nazi Germany and its associated anti-Semitism has made it impossible to use it in other contexts, except perhaps in India.
- The cross is so associated with Christianity and in Muslim countries with the Crusaders, that it is impossible to use it as a sign of neutral medical help. Muslim states use the red crescent symbol as an alternative to the red cross. The international Red Cross organisation has now devised a totally neutral symbol to replace the cross in some cultural contexts.

4.3 Organisation and combination of signs

Signs are organised into **codes**, from which selections are made to construct meaningful combinations — in much the same way as words are chosen for meaningful sentences. These combinations can be in visual media (paintings, advertisements and posters of films) and also in any other cultural medium, from architecture to dress and appearance. For example, an architect can select from the various design elements that compose a building to create a gothic, classical, baroque, modern or post-modern style.

Choices from particular codes are called **paradigms**, where one unit is chosen to fit into a chain (or **syntagm**) to form a whole. For example, in a woman's wardrobe a choice can be made from hats, tops, skirts, trousers and shoes to form the look of an outfit, but she can only wear one of each element at any time. If you change the hat or the shoes, you change the look or meaning of the whole outfit.

4.4 Application of semiotics to cultural artefacts

- Semiotic techniques and analysis can be applied to any cultural artefact, from a film or poster to a style of dress or even a dinner menu.
- The meaning of the combinations or syntagms is culturally determined and subject to variation and change.
- Understanding of syntagms is subjective and dependent on the cultural background of individuals, and the contextual value system and codes of the culture from which they arise.

- The meaning of any particular image is subjective — it is dependent on the audience's background knowledge, beliefs and expectations and therefore open to wide interpretation, unless the image is **anchored** by a caption or in some other way to limit the field of interpretation.
- The placing of images next to each other creates a syntagm for the viewer. For example, a photograph of a dead body followed by one of a man holding a gun suggests that the man is the killer.

4.5 Useful words in semiotics

Bricolage: the mixing together of different elements — whether images, signs or physical objects — to create new cultural meanings. It is often associated with youth cultures, such as skinheads' use of Doc Martens work boots, old fashioned braces, Ben Sherman shirts and military crew cuts to create a distinctive uniform to signal group membership.

Anchorage: the process whereby a visual image is explained or interpreted by a written caption in such a way as to limit the possible meanings attributable to the image — for example, a photograph of diseased lungs with the caption 'smoking kills'.

Denotation: the first or simplest level of meaning; a photograph of a rose denotes or represents the rose flower.

Connotation: the second cultural or symbolic level of meaning, where a photograph of a rose can mean many things: passion, female beauty or England.

Myth: a persistent belief, based on the constant repetition of particular representations by the media. Cultural myths become embedded, sometimes working on a subconscious level, and can be used as a framework for advertisements. The countryside as a wholesome, traditional, healthy, reliable and honest environment is a useful backdrop for Anchor butter, Baxters soups and wholemeal bread, all of which are the products of a factory conveyor belt. The myth of the English countryside was seriously challenged by images of burning mounds of dead cattle during the foot and mouth epidemic.

Field of interpretation: possible meanings of an image that are different from that intended by the image maker. This can be limited by the process known as **anchorage**, illustrated in Figure 1. An image is subject to a wide range of meanings when viewed by an audience — a 'field of interpretation'. The intended meaning of an image can be 'anchored', i.e. firmly tied down, by means of the elements illustrated in the diagram.

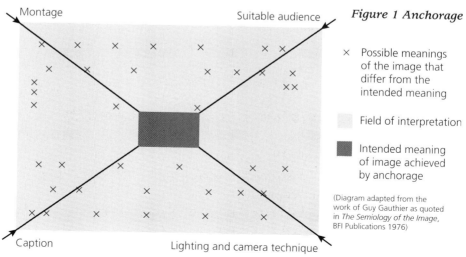

Figure 1 Anchorage

× Possible meanings of the image that differ from the intended meaning

Field of interpretation

Intended meaning of image achieved by anchorage

(Diagram adapted from the work of Guy Gauthier as quoted in *The Semiology of the Image*, BFI Publications 1976)

4.6 Application of semiology to the visual image

Semiotic terms can be used when analysing print material, such as magazine adverts and posters, or the moving image:

Adverts: the whole ad is a syntagm made up of the paradigmatic choices of elements — for example, the subject being advertised, the location, setting and context, the colour palette, iconography and captions.

Film posters: these need to suggest the whole film experience to a potential viewer and select elements accordingly which — apart from images of celebrity stars and scenes from the film — might also include special features, director and cast awards from film festivals, quotations from favourable critics, and sound and other technical credits, together with a scene that **metonymically** represents the whole film experience and is sometimes accompanied by an anchoring strapline, such as 'In space no-one can hear you scream', which was used in *Alien* (Ridley Scott 1979).

Films and television productions: these can be analysed using semiotic terms. The whole film is a syntagm, or montage, of individual scenes that represent the paradigmatic choices of the director, including the choice of film stock, colour palette, type of shot, actors and mise-en-scène.

TERMINOLOGY

Metonym: the representation of the whole by a part, for example a photograph of a policeman being attacked by two youths could be used by a newspaper to represent a riot involving 5000 people.

EXAMINER'S TIP

Try to work the language of semiology naturally into your analysis of text. For example, a Valentine's card with a picture of a red rose and the caption 'Forever yours' could be described as follows:

The picture of the rose denotes the rose flower and could have various meanings. However, the anchoring caption 'Forever yours' limits the field of interpretation and reinforces the connotation of love and passion associated with the flower and the colour red. Roses are traditionally associated with Valentine's Day and have developed mythic significance.

This chapter covers textual analysis and explores the subject matter as defined by the OCR and AQA examination boards.

1 *Specification focus: OCR Unit 2731 (AS), Section B*

OCR Unit 2731 is divided into two parts, with the second half of the exam involving a compulsory question based on the comparative study of two texts chosen by centres from a choice of prescribed genres. These include:

* **consumerism** and **lifestyle magazines**
* celebrity and the tabloid press
* music culture and radio
* gender and television situation comedy

This list is subject to addition and alteration by the examining board, so be sure to check the options for your particular examination year.

The focus of the compulsory question is on the key concept of **representation**.

1.1 Consumerism and lifestyle magazines

Consumerism: a variation of capitalism whereby the economy is kept buoyant by the encouragement of high levels of personal consumption of goods and services. The system is sustained by personal spending and the ready availability of credit, and is stimulated by advertising and marketing strategies in relation to individual lifestyles. Goods and services are associated with lifestyles promoted by the advertising and marketing industries.

Lifestyle: a marketing term, whereby individuals are targeted by advertisers through reference to their particular way of life and pattern of consumption. For example, alcohol, trainers, sportswear, popular music and films are often targeted at teenagers, whereas second homes, holidays and health care insurance are more likely to be targeted at the older generation.

Lifestyle magazines: magazines that provide an audience for advertisers, based on an age and gender profile, aspirations and patterns of consumption. Examples include *Loaded*, *FHM*, *Marie Claire*, *Sugar*, *Cosmopolitan* and *Bliss*.

Questions and answers

Q: How do lifestyle magazines attract their readership?

A: By having attractive covers, using **teasers** to draw readers in and often using photographs of celebrities known to the readership. Idealised versions of life show representations of the target audience surrounded by the acquired desirable products of a consumer lifestyle. Magazines make themselves look attractive by using an appropriate mode of address and by including articles that engage with the readers' attitudes, beliefs, values and daily interests and concerns.

Q: What kind of representations dominate lifestyle magazines?

A: Usually glamorous and perfected people, models, famous and successful individuals and exotic places. Representations often provide idealised role models for the target audience.

Q: What representations are not present?

A: Usually the poor, the unattractive, the sick, the old and the unsuccessful. There are often limited representations of ethnic minorities. For example, in Britain, with a

growing population of people of southeast Asian, Chinese and Japanese origin, there are very few representations of this ethnicity in lifestyle and fashion magazines.

Q: *What is the target audience for the magazine and how is this reflected in the content?*

A: The target audience should be obvious from the images used on the cover, the language register and mode of address, and the nature of advertisements and articles. For a title like *FHM*, the photograph of an attractive, semi-naked female on the cover, advertisements for aftershave and trainers, and articles on a boys' night out all suggest a lad's magazine aimed at 16–30 year olds.

Q: *What are the products advertised and how do they relate to the articles?*

A: The advertisements will be focused on the products that the target audience could be expected to purchase. A magazine for teenage girls is likely to include adverts for cosmetics, perfume, shampoo, clothes and accessories. Many of the articles themselves are often little more than recommendations of particular products.

Q: *What percentage of the magazine is taken up by advertisements?*

A: This is always larger than you think. In the September 2005 edition of *Marie Claire* magazine, 273 out of 387 pages were advertisements or advertising features — approximately 70% of the magazine.

EXAMINER'S TIP

Always remember that lifestyle and consumer magazines provide audiences for advertisers who make the magazine profitable to produce. Without advertising, the magazines would not exist.

TERMINOLOGY

Teaser: a device designed to attract and retain the attention of an audience, in the hope that it will consume more of the product on offer. In print media, a teaser is a combination of words or phrases on a magazine cover or newspaper front page, designed to entice the reader to the publication.

1.2 Celebrity and the tabloid press

TERMINOLOGY

Celebrity: an individual who has become the focus of media attention and is therefore widely known and recognised by the public. Celebrities may be associated with a particular career, lifestyle or activity (e.g. top fashion models, music stars and footballers) but increasingly can be ordinary individuals with no particular skills or talent, made famous by media coverage, such as the Big Brother contestants.

Tabloid press: British newspapers of tabloid size producing popular journalism with a low intellectual content, aimed at a readership of C2, D and E social class brackets. Tabloids concentrate on human-interest storylines, with an emphasis on the private lives of celebrities at the expense of serious coverage of hard news items.

Questions and answers

Q: *What is a celebrity?*

A: Any person identified by the media as being of interest for whatever reason. Attention paid by the media to people and their activities, however mundane, has the effect of turning them into celebrities — for example, Chantelle Houghton, winner of *Celebrity Big Brother* in 2006, was a fake celebrity.

Q: How are celebrities represented?

A: As objects of admiration, envy and condemnation, depending on the aspect of their lives and behaviour attracting media attention. They are role models and measures of the social acceptability of certain kinds of behaviour. For example, tabloid newspaper headlines in March 2006 drew attention to statistics indicating a dramatic increase in cocaine use among schoolchildren; a photograph of model Kate Moss was used to illustrate the front page article, as she had previously been identified as a cocaine user and therefore a negative role model for the young. The implication of the association was that Moss, increasingly criticised by the tabloids, was partly responsible for making cocaine use seem more acceptable to the young.

Q: What is the relationship between celebrities and the tabloid press?

A: The tabloid press exploits celebrity recognition and popularity to increase newspaper sales. Celebrities often welcome publicity if it improves their career prospects or raises public awareness of them, but they resent it when it draws attention to their excesses, shortcomings, marital disputes and failures.

Q: Whose interests do these relationships serve?

A: Both parties.

Q: Why are readers interested in the lives of celebrities?

A: Celebrities represent idealised individuals. They are often wealthy, with all the freedom of life choices that wealth brings. Those who are obsessed with celebrities often see them as role models with whom they can identify and whose lifestyle they envy. The intrusive nature of media attention makes readers feel that they personally know the celebrities, which creates a false intimacy. Readers also enjoy seeing them brought down to earth as a form of moral retribution for their failures and excesses.

Q: How does tabloid coverage create celebrities?

A: Simply by focusing on them, making their behaviour seem significant and projecting their image to a mass audience. If individuals are known and recognised, they become valuable to advertisers and media producers because they can be used to draw attention to products and programmes. Celebrities often use **publicists** to help further their careers.

Q: How can tabloid coverage enhance the careers of celebrities?

A: Simply by providing them with publicity, thereby making them better known and more attractive to advertisers and media producers.

Q: Why do tabloids so often emphasise the ups and downs of relationships, broken marriages, affairs, scandals involving drink and drugs, and violent or disorderly behaviour?

A: Because this is part of a 'rise and fall' morality where individuals are elevated by the media and public interest, receive all the benefits of a luxury lifestyle, and are then brought down by their own behaviour. It is a form of moral retribution and *Schadenfreude* (a German word meaning to take pleasure in the misfortune of others).

TERMINOLOGY

Publicist: an individual who manages the public relations and profile of an individual in the public eye. A publicist usually operates by manipulating press stories to create a more positive image and by suppressing negative storylines. The high-profile publicist Max Clifford is quoted as saying: 'the biggest part of my job is stopping stories'.

Notoriety can be an attractive commodity for celebrities. Newspaper coverage often creates ambiguous moral responses. In 2005, supermodel Kate Moss was photographed taking cocaine and associating with rock and roll bad boy Pete Docherty, and these photographs appeared in tabloid newspapers. After universal condemnation, she was interviewed by police and forced to make a public apology, and for a short period her contracts with some major perfume and couture producers were suspended. However, within 2 months she was back on the cover of *Vogue* magazine. Kate Moss is currently the highest paid model in the world and has doubled her earnings to £9 million a year. In 2006, she signed a new contract with Calvin Kline worth £500,000.

1.3 Music culture and radio

Origins of music culture

Modern music culture progressed alongside the development of radio. The recording industry has always been reflective of social class and cultural and racial differences. The cultural appeal of black music and jazz in the twentieth century was that it challenged mainstream ideology and dominant, bourgeois music forms such as classical music and broadly based popular music.

Jazz was good-time music and from its start had connotations of sexual promiscuity and experimentation (it was sometimes referred to as 'whorehouse music'). Blues reflected social deprivation, exclusion, racial discrimination and the marginalisation of the black community in America. Folk and country music recorded the working practices and life experience of ordinary communities.

The fusion of the energy of jazz with the critical angst of the blues developed as a popular form and was the essence of the music of the emerging youth culture in the post-war period of the 1940s and 1950s, further developing through rock and roll to produce the teenage music and cultural revolution of the 1960s.

During this period, social and economic factors, which were a combination of increased prosperity and the relaxing of social constraints, gave birth to an assertive teenage culture with its own hip, cryptic language, developed from jazz talk. This language challenged mainstream values, and its proponents engaged in sexual experimentation, were committed to pleasure seeking and used musical expression as the background text.

From the early days, there has been a debate between populists and purists in the music business. If jazz, blues, folk and country music were seen as pure forms embedded in the communities from which they were drawn, then popular music (even rock and roll) was seen as the music industry's commercial exploitation of these forms, adapting, taming and marketing them to a wide audience through the mass communication media of disc and radio. This debate continues with disc jockeys being accused of serving the commercial interests of record producers by giving airtime to favoured bands and music styles at the expense of raw talent and originality.

Music and radio

* Music has been a major part of radio output since the early days of the BBC, with classical music being offered on the BBC's Third Programme (1946–67), popular music on the Light Programme (1945–67) and dance band music on the Home

Service (1939–67). The division reflected the distinction between 'high brow' (classical) and 'low brow' (popular) music forms.

- The popularity of American big band music during the Second World War and the development of swing, jive and the jitterbug paved the way for the post-war music scene.

- The post-war period saw the development of 'pop' — short for popular — and the subsequent emergence of rock and roll.

- Rock and roll music culture became associated with teenage rebellion and the growth of sub-cultures (e.g. Teddy Boys, Mods and Rockers). BBC radio devoted only limited airtime to the new music and its slow response to cultural change meant that Radio Luxembourg (broadcasting from Europe) and pirate radio stations broadcasting on boats moored off the British coast and outside territorial waters (e.g. Radio Caroline 1964–67), filled the gap. The pirates were overwhelmed by a combination of government legislation outlawing the stations and the reshaping of BBC radio output in line with current taste in music in the form of Radio 1 (launched in 1967).

- The establishment of commercial radio in 1974 greatly increased the number of stations available, and the deregulation of broadcasting in the 1980s and 1990s further diversified the range of stations available, with an increasing emphasis on ethnic and local broadcasting.

- Radio is important in the development and dissemination of music culture, as music not played on radio often goes unheard; consequently, DJs are under pressure from record companies to promote their products.

- Music downloads from the internet, and the growth of iPods and MP3 players, are challenging the dominant role of radio in directing musical tastes by controlling output.

Questions and answers

Q: How does radio create a market for a particular style of music?

A: Simply by pushing the records and constantly hyping the musicians concerned.

Q: What kind of music is favoured by radio stations?

A: Usually highly commercial music backed by major producers with big marketing budgets.

Q: What music is excluded and why?

A: Alternative music with a small audience, which is not promoted by the major companies.

Q: Does radio encourage new talent, originality and creativity in the music business?

A: Only to the extent that certain DJs and stations may make a point of targeting minority interests and playing lesser-known bands. This remains a small percentage of total radio output.

Q: What part do institutions like the multinational conglomerates (who own recording companies) play in generating and popularising musical styles and performers?

A: A large part, as the funds they have at their disposal can make or break new performers. Their interests are solely commercial and if they spot a talent that can make money they will make a commercial decision to market it.

Q: How is radio threatened by the developments in the internet and the emergence of iPods and MP3 players?

A: Radio is only one way of accessing music, and individuals can now exercise greater freedom of choice by using internet technology and storing and accessing their music library through portable media players.

1.4 Gender and television situation comedy

Gender can be defined as the psychological and cultural aspects of behaviour associated with masculinity and femininity, acquired through socialisation, in accordance with the expectations of a particular society.

Situation comedy

A situation comedy (or sitcom) is a television or radio comedy in which the characters are located in particular contained environments that form the basis of their relationship and the centre of the action.

Gender patterns in situation comedy

- Frustrated, competitive males with no resident females: *The Young Ones, Steptoe and Son, Frasier, Men Behaving Badly*
- Young males trying to establish themselves in life and seeking success with women: *The Likely Lads*
- Resident females with no resident males: *Absolutely Fabulous*, *The Liver Birds*
- Resident males and females in complex relationships: *Friends*
- Domestic harmony/disharmony and male/female incompatibility for the purpose of comedy: *Terry and June*, *Sykes*, *The Dick Van Dyke Show*, *The Good Life*, *Bewitched*
- Old age and domestic disharmony as comedy: *One Foot in the Grave*
- Sexual frustration/abstinence and lonely people: *Rising Damp*
- Father and son in constant battle, with son's attempts to better himself being thwarted by his father: *Steptoe and Son*
- Sexual ambiguity/homosexuality: *Are You Being Served?*
- Stereotyped working class gender relationships: *The Royle Family*, *Till Death Us do Part*
- Frustrated, foolish and nostalgic old men getting into trouble and trying to stay young, while hopelessly failing with the opposite sex: *Last of the Summer Wine*
- Male and female flatmates whose friendship is compromised by the fact that the female's ex-boyfriend is the male's best friend: *Not Going Out* (2006).
- Typical British family relations, with arguments and everyday issues presented as comedy: *My Family* (2000–).

Questions to apply to the comedies being studied

- To what extent is the source of comedy reliant on stereotypes, gender relations and expectations?
- To what extent is sexual frustration or failure with the opposite sex the source of the comedy?
- Does the situation comedy challenge or reinforce existing gender stereotypes and expectations?
- What representations are present and are they positive or negative?
- Do the narratives have a circular form, where the characters make no progress in their condition and are left as we find them?
- How is comedy used to address serious gender issues between men and women?

2 *Specification focus: AQA Unit 2 (AS)*

AQA Unit 2 offers four choices of textual topics as areas of study, from which centres choose two:

- film and broadcast fiction
- documentary

  ‣ advertising and marketing
  ‣ British newspapers

2.1 Film and broadcast fiction

Film

This unit requires the analysis and discussion of film texts and knowledge of the language of film according to the key concepts. Questions on film require you to focus on the techniques used to construct the film text within a specific genre and the characteristics of that genre.

When revising the films you have watched and prepared for the examination you should concentrate on the following aspects:

- **genre** and genre conventions, including iconography, and how these are followed or adapted in the films you have studied
- **representations** of characters and places
- **narrative** development and themes
- **film language** — the techniques used by the film maker
- **audience appeal** — how does the film attract and retain the interest of an audience?

An example is the film *Titanic* (James Cameron 1997). The sinking of the Cunard White Star liner *Titanic* in 1912, following its collision with an iceberg, has formed the basis of several films recreating the tragedy. James Cameron's film involved a record-breaking budget and proved to be a tremendous commercial success.

- **Genre:** disaster/romance hybrid, with links to contemporary documentary and exploiting a strong interest in the exploration of the lost ship. The period re-enactment of the sinking is a well-tried formula, with at least three earlier versions. This version, with its huge budget, recreated an accurate model of the ship, a third of its actual size. Computer-generated imagery was used to portray the sinking, with blue screen technology used to convey the sailing of the ship. There is a symbiotic dimension, with the release of Celine Dion's multi-million dollar hit *My Heart Will Go On* as the theme song of the film.

- **Representations:** many new fictional characters are introduced, with Rose and Jack as the focus of romance, using Kate Winslet and Leonardo DiCaprio. Some historical characters, such as Captain Smith and the shipbuilder Mr Andrews, act out historical dialogue. The main characters are young and come across as modern by their challenge of the rigid social attitudes of 1912; this helps contemporary audiences relate to the plot. The surviving character, Rose, is represented as a twentieth-century heroine, a New Woman with strong appeal to a female audience, surviving the disaster by overcoming the grief of a lost love and living a full and varied life. As an old woman she provides the living link to the disaster and the current exploration of the wreck. Her death in the closing moments of the film, and the ghostly sequence that follows, completes the narrative by returning her symbolically to the wreck to rejoin her long-lost lover.

- **Narrative strands** follow the contemporary search for the famous lost ship in the opening scenes, followed by a flashback to 1912 and the princess and pauper romance between Rose (1st class) and Jack (3rd or steerage class), at the expense of Rose's upper-middle-class fiancé, played as a villain. The film provides a concentrated version of a twentieth-century class war, with traditional class divisions being swept away by love and ultimately by tragedy. Underpinning all is the disaster movie scenario of rising water in the sinking ship. The iceberg interrupts the romance narrative.

- **Audience:** this film appeals to multiple audiences, with its mix of disaster movie/historical re-enactment/teen romance/young stars. There is a reassuringly predictable outcome — the ship sinks — but Jack's death from hypothermia in the freezing water when he had survived the sinking adds a tragically unexpected twist to the audience's expectations.

Broadcast fiction

The examples of broadcast fiction studied will be dependent on your centre's choice, but the distinctive nature of television as a medium will feature in your analysis.

Distinctive features of broadcast fiction

- Television is an intimate medium, received in the home by individuals and small groups of people.
- Conventional television receivers (other than large home cinema screens) are more suited to intimate, close-up camera work than to epic, large-scale landscapes and distance shots.
- Broadcast fiction can create a regular audience for two- or three-part dramas with recognisable locations and characters, or longer series presented as part of an evening's entertainment.
- Television fiction on commercial channels is constructed episodically around advertising breaks and often includes a recap element when the break is over.
- Viewers are free to come and go during the transmission and can record and replay the transmission or change channel midway through.
- Writers of television fiction need to create characters who are easily recognisable within a short space of time. The increasingly popular practice of 'channel-hopping' makes it harder to retain viewers and increases the need to introduce dramatic tension points regularly in order to hold the audience's interest.

2.2 Documentary

A documentary is any film made about real life as opposed to a fictional construct.

Origins of documentary

The term 'documentary' was first used by the film maker John Grierson, and his film *Drifters* (1929) is usually cited as the first of the genre. Robert Flaherty made *Nanook of the North* in 1922, an account of the daily life of a group of Inuit Eskimos living on Hudson's Bay in Canada, by filming the Inuit and organising his footage into a coherent narrative. Films of this kind were known as **travelogues** and were clearly early documentaries.

Characteristics of documentaries

- Because they are filmed versions of real life, documentaries are seen as having merit as accurate records of real people and real events, places, lifestyles and working practices.
- In reality, documentaries are based on selection, construction and editing, just like any other film.
- They have a powerful impact on audiences, who see them as being true to life, and therefore they are effective tools of propaganda and social action.
- Documentary/news reportage techniques were used by Soviet and Nazi propaganda machines in the 1930s. Examples include the work of German film maker Leni Riefenstahl in *Triumph des Willens* ('Triumph of the Will'), showing a Nazi Party rally in Nuremburg, and *Olympia* (a film of the 1936 Berlin Olympics, released in 1938).

- In Britain during the Second World War, the Crown Film Unit was responsible to the Ministry of Information for producing morale-boosting propaganda films such as *Britain Can Take It* (Humphrey Jennings and Harry Watt 1940) and *Listen to Britain* (Humphrey Jennings 1942).
- Documentaries were originally made for the cinema but adapted well to television.
- Traditional documentary often included a male voice of authority to provide the commentary.

Documentary today

- The general availability of the video camera and editing software has made filming 'real life' open to all. Ordinary people can make and appear in home-made documentaries.
- Traditional documentary style is no longer popular with television audiences, and this has led to a more sensational and personalised documentary style, such as the hidden camera investigations of the fashion industry by Donal McIntyre (see also the discussion of docu-soaps on p. 48).
- Television series such as *You Are What you Eat*, *It's Me or the Dog* and *Brat Camp* (Channel 4) and the 'video diary' approach adopted by many programmes are in the documentary tradition; they reflect a shift away from the formal authoritative voice in favour of a more audience-friendly, relaxed and involved style of presentation.
- Reality television using ordinary people in carefully managed situations is a form of documentary.

EXAMINER'S TIP

Remember that documentaries are no more real than any other constructed media text — they just seem more real. Real life is real life — all media texts are just versions of it.

Social realism

- Social realism involves the use of actors in realistic everyday situations, often re-enacting actual events and characters.
- Camera techniques are naturalistic and designed to create a sense of the everyday. Lighting and sound systems are also rudimentary and naturalistic to give the impression that what is being filmed is just the usual experience.
- Classic examples include *Cathy Come Home* (Ken Loach 1966), *A Taste of Honey* (Tony Richardson 1961), *Kes* (Ken Loach 1970) and *Sweet Sixteen* (Ken Loach 2003).

Social action cinema

This refers to films that use a documentary approach to draw attention to an issue of social concern, with the intention of raising public awareness and bringing about social reform. For example, public concern over homelessness following the TV showing of *Cathy Come Home* (Ken Loach 1966), which highlighted the problems, led to the foundation of the charity Shelter.

Historical reconstruction

This term applies to films that aim to reproduce actual historical events as closely and as accurately as possible, using real characters, dialogues and situations. Examples include: *Downfall* (Oliver Hirschbiegel 2005), which reconstructs the last days of Adolf Hitler and the fall of Berlin to the Russians in 1945; *Bloody Sunday* (Paul Greengrass

2002), which recreates the shooting of Irish civilians by British soldiers during the Northern Ireland conflict; and *United 93* (Paul Greengrass 2006), which reconstructs events on one of the planes involved in the 9/11 terrorist attacks on the USA.

Docu-soap

- A docu-soap is a documentary series filmed in the style of a soap opera, with a range of real characters being followed through their everyday experiences.
- Traditional documentaries, seen as serious and educational, are not popular with mass television audiences, so the genre has adapted to provide entertainment hybrids that are often cheap to produce but without any serious social purpose.
- Examples in 2006 include *Airport*, *Boot Camp*, *Neighbours from Hell*, *Wife Swap* and *How Clean is Your House?*

2.3 Advertising and marketing

Advertising is the media-led promotion of goods or services for sale, whereby audiences are brought to the market and encouraged or persuaded to consume.

The advertising agency

This is a company or firm engaged in the production of advertising and marketing materials, in response to briefs developed with clients.

In a sophisticated media environment, advertising agencies play an important role in assessing the attitudes, beliefs and values of audiences and in relating campaigns to current social, cultural and political trends.

Skilled and creative professional teams ensure that powerful and lasting images of products and their place in contemporary life are projected to audiences so that such images become part of their everyday cultural experience. The concept of **brand** is crucial to successful advertising, and agencies concentrate on building brands in an increasingly competitive market.

Major worldwide agencies include Ogilvy and Mather, J. Walter Thompson, McCann-Erickson, BBDO Starcom, MediaVest, MindShare, OMD, Young and Rubicam, Bartle Bogle Hegarty, and Saatchi and Saatchi.

Control of Advertising

The Advertising Standards Authority (ASA)

This is the body established by the Advertising Association (the advertising industry trade federation) in 1962 to oversee the self-regulation of the advertising industry.

Its principal requirement is that advertisements should be 'legal, decent, honest and truthful'. Its code of practice is a practical alternative to proposed restrictive government legislation and it publishes a monthly journal on issues and complaints relating to the contents of adverts.

The Independent Television Commission (ITC)

The ITC regulates the content and frequency of advertising on independent television. This includes ITV, Channel 4, Five, and satellite broadcasters such as Sky. Its Code of Advertising Standards and Practice works in conjunction with that of the ASA.

The ITC's provisions include the requirement that advertisements should not:
- give misleading descriptions of products
- make unwarranted claims about products

- make claims that alcoholic drinks enhance social or sexual success
- contain **subliminal** messages
- be used for political purposes
- be confused with programmes
- encourage dangerous driving
- offend against good taste and decency

Subliminal advertising: this works on a subconscious level by introducing barely perceptible messages into other media texts and thereby influencing consumers without their realising it. This can involve flashing images on a screen for a fraction of a second, or the insertion of sound track messages in audio transmissions.

Lifestyle marketing

This is the presentation of goods for sale within the context of a total way of life.

The four Cs

This term was used by the advertising agency Young & Rubicam in the 1980s to describe categories of consumers identified by the agency as being the new focus of their campaign strategies. The categories are:

- **achievers** — those people who have achieved career and financial success and are at the top of their profession. They are high spenders on luxury and quality goods and expect the best of everything, from home furnishings to cars and food products. However, they do not need to display their wealth and success too obviously as they are quietly confident of their achievements. The following top-of-the-range products would be aimed at them: Rolls-Royce, Mercedes and BMW cars, Colefax and Fowler wallpapers, Fortnum and Mason tea and Saville Row suits.
- **aspirers** — those people who are trying to improve themselves and who use consumer goods as status symbols to represent their aspirational status. Products aimed at this category could include Rolex watches, Porsche cars and 4×4s, fashionable designer labels like Paul Smith, and state-of-the-art kitchen and hi-fi gadgets.
- **mainstreamers** — this category is of people who need to feel comfortable and secure in the impression that they are like others. They seek reassurance and reliability in household names and famous brands — for example, Marks and Spencer for everything, including home furnishings. They deliberately choose branded goods like Heinz baked beans and Daz washing powder.
- **reformers** — these are usually confident, well-educated individuals, often with careers in the social services or education. They are resistant to consumer advertising and follow their own instincts, tending to choose supermarket own brands, whole foods, organic meat and vegetables, fair trade coffee and tea, Habitat furniture, functional and reliable transport such as Volkswagen cars, diesel rather than petrol and recycled children's clothes.

The four Cs approach was significant because it signalled a move away from traditional social class and income bracketing of consumers and recognised that lifestyle aspirations and the use of products to create a sense of personal identity was becoming more important in the lives of consumers.

Lifestage

This is an advertising and marketing term used in lifestyle analysis, based on the idea that people have different tastes and aspirations at different stages of their lives. Lifestages can be categorised as follows:

- **dependents** — those dependent on other people's money, for example children and students supported by their parents
- **empty-nesters:** adults whose children have left home
- **pre-family:** young couples without children
- **DINKs** (dual income no kids) — couples with no children and a large disposable income
- **grey market:** pensioners with significant financial assets and few financial commitments

Branding

Branding is a form of marketing that seeks to identify a product, idea or individual as having specific characteristics that constitute a unique and separate identity and desirable qualities that are offered to consumers.

Brand identity can be associated with a range of products — for example, the Marlboro brand, with its trademark masculine, outdoor, rugged appeal, has been successfully transferred from the declining cigarette market to the flourishing fashion market. Fashion houses like Armani can also transfer their brand to sunglasses and perfumes. The Virgin brand created by Richard Branson began with records at the beginning of the 1970s and has since been applied to an airline, trains, mobile phones, digital, financial and motoring services, and a chain of Megastores.

Celebrity and lifestyle

A celebrity is an individual who has become the focus of media attention and is therefore widely known and recognised by the public.

- Celebrities may be associated with a particular career, lifestyle or activity, such as football, pop music, modelling or the film industry. Increasingly, celebrities can be ordinary individuals who become famous and often wealthy as a result of their lives and personalities being publicised by the media.
- The key to being a celebrity is recognition by the public and a lifestyle that attracts public interest.
- Although they have no real authority, the opinions and life choices of celebrities are extremely influential and can be exploited by advertisers.
- Celebrities are often presented as brands associated with, and endorsing, a range of products, such as David Beckham's brand of cool masculinity, which can be associated with clothes, razors, trainers and mobile phones.

EXAMINER'S TIP

Remember that celebrities are involved in the construction of their own brand identity and that all coverage of their activities serves to endorse this identity. Being in the news, regardless of the type of coverage, is essential to them if they are to sell themselves. The real truth behind published stories is irrelevant, as are the often emotional and highly publicised reactions of those they concern, because celebrities have chosen to turn their lives into living soap operas as a way of staying in the public eye and making money.

Point for discussion

Anthony Giddens is a sociologist of late modernity who has studied the democratisation of all aspects of life. He argues that we are no longer given our identity through inheritance or socialisation but that we create it through a process of construction. We constantly work on our 'self' and seek to express who we are through the adoption of lifestyles represented in the media. These representations play an important part in helping us to structure and review our identity and to make personal decisions about ourselves, our relationships and the world around us. Celebrities provide role models against whom we can measure our achievements.

2.4 British newspapers

These are classified as quality or tabloid as a means of describing their audience and approach to the news. The **ABC1 scale** (see p. 8) is used to classify media audiences and in particular to distinguish between the readership of tabloid and quality newspapers. It is also used by advertisers as one method of identifying audience profiles and different market segments.

Newspapers and politics

All newspapers are produced within an ideological framework and offer commentaries on social, cultural, political and economic affairs, with editorials that advance the point of view of the editor and proprietor, often with political opinions and preferences expressed. At election time, newspapers line up in support of individual politicians, parties and policies, usually with predetermined allegiances.

Areas of public concern subject to political debate in newspapers

- The National Health Service
- Crime, punishment and the legal system
- Foreign policy and war
- The European Union
- The honesty, trustworthiness and competence of politicians
- Taxation and income levels, economic competence and the state of the economy
- Education policy
- Social welfare policy and equal opportunities
- Housing
- Unemployment levels
- Immigration and asylum policy

Importance of these areas

These areas are pressure points for any government and become the battleground of political debate during elections. The newspaper agenda on these areas will depend on which party they support and whether the area is one of strength or weakness for the government.

Newspapers and values

Newspapers reflect the attitudes, beliefs and values of their readership and the society in which they are produced. These values are, in turn, reflected in political beliefs and alignments. It is therefore important to have an understanding of the terminology used to describe the major political groupings and ideologies.

New College Nottingham
Learning Centres

Political terminology

The use of political terminology is complicated by the many changes in the policies, positioning and ideology of the recognised political parties, and some would argue that many of the traditional terms explained below are no longer relevant to British politics for the following reasons:

- Politicians increasingly offer populist packages pitched at the public by media-friendly personalities, which have little or no ideological content and differ only in their presentation and not in their substance.
- Politicians are marketed as 'celebrities', in and out of favour with the media and easily exchangeable for new faces when their popularity falters.
- Politicians who are physically unappealing and perform poorly for the media have little chance of sustaining or even reaching high office.
- Manipulating media presentation of policies and personalities through communication managers and 'spin doctors' has become a major aspect of any political party's effort to achieve power.

Conservatism: belief in the importance of the freedom of the individual to create wealth in a society for the benefit of all, and in the need to maintain existing institutions and traditions, such as the family and the monarchy, in the face of demands for radical change. These beliefs are usually expressed by support for the Conservative Party.

Socialism: belief that it is the duty of the state to take measures to break down social class barriers and ensure the provision of equal opportunities and the fair distribution of wealth for all in a society. This means that the state involves itself directly with the national economy and the means of production, through public ownership or nationalisation of major industries and public services such as the health service. Unlike communism, which advocates change through revolution, democratic socialism advocates change on a gradual consensual basis through the ballot box. These beliefs were traditionally expressed by support for the Labour Party.

New Labour: the term coined by Labour Party election strategists to signal a move away from traditional socialist principles (like the public ownership of major industries) in pursuit of more populist policies, following an 18-year period in opposition. The so-called 'third way' associated with the party's 1997 election victory represented a continuation of many previous Conservative government policies but with increased public expenditure on the health and education services.

Left wing: in support of the socialist or Labour Party.

Liberal: the term traditionally used for supporters of the Liberal Party (in Britain now called the Liberal Democrats). Liberal policies are not anchored to party dogma and tend to be more freethinking and radical, particularly in social matters.

Liberal (USA): this term has different meanings in America, where it is associated with permissive social policies and is often used as a term of abuse by right-wing politicians to imply weakness or softness on issues like crime levels, the death penalty, abortion, sexual misconduct and drug abuse.

Liberal (economic context): in an economic context, the term implies opposition to state control and government regulation of national economies. Liberal economists, sometimes called free market capitalists, are against the protection of national economies through trade barriers such as tariffs and import quotas, and believe that market forces alone should be left to determine the relationship between the supply, demand and price of goods and services in a globalised market.

Progressive: a view of society that sees social change and evolution as positive and desirable.

Radical: a belief in dramatic change and a break with tradition.

Reactionary: resistant to social change and desiring the maintenance of traditional conservative values and beliefs.

Fascism: a term derived from the anti-communist right-wing Italian nationalist party, led by Benito Mussolini, who was in power in Italy from 1922 to 1943. The term was used to describe similar movements in Germany, Spain and elsewhere. It is now loosely applied to any nationalist, authoritarian, repressive, right-wing politics, sometimes with racist connotations. In Britain, the extreme right-wing British National Party (BNP) is often described as 'fascist', although this term is rejected by its supporters.

Communism: belief in the views of Karl Marx, principally that capitalist society involves the exploitation of the working class by the ruling class and that, through a process of class awareness, struggle and revolution, the more numerous working class will eventually seize the means of production and build a classless, socialist society. In the medium term, a dictatorship of the proletariat would involve the control of all the means of production and distribution by an authoritarian state. The system was applied in Russia following the 1917 revolution by Lenin (who died in 1924) and subsequently Stalin (who died in 1953), and it lasted until the collapse of the Soviet Union in the late 1980s. The Chinese People's Republic is still nominally the largest communist power in the world, although it developed its own version of a capitalist economy during the 1990s. In Britain, there is limited support for both the Communist Party and extreme left-wing groups such as the Socialist Workers Party; these have become little more than minority pressure groups.

Fringe politics: this is a term used for small groups outside the political mainstream and often without any clear left/right tradition. Extreme socialist and fascist groups could be described as fringe, as could single issue groups like the Animal Liberation Front and supporters of Islamic revolutionary groups.

Pressure groups: these are groups who seek to exert pressure on the government to introduce particular measures or adopt particular policies. They include Greenpeace, Friends of the Earth, War on Want, Age Concern, Ash, the League Against Cruel Sports, the Countryside Alliance, the Anti-Vivisection League, the Society for the Protection of Unborn Children, and the Muslim Council of Britain. By focusing on a single issue or representing a specific minority, these groups can be extremely influential as they target MPs and cultivate the media. At a time when individual involvement with mainstream political parties is in decline, these groups are exerting increasing influence on government policy, decision making and legislation.

Centre politics: a term used to describe the middle or common ground between left- and right-wing views, increasingly sought by politicians seeking electoral success. The crowding of this middle ground, with similar policies produced by different parties, makes distinguishing between the parties increasingly difficult for the electorate.

The election in 2005 of David Cameron as leader of the Conservative Party has led to an even greater similarity between the pitch of the two principal parties, with Cameron seeking to attract mainstream New Labour supporters.

CHAPTER 3

Feel good factor

The creation of a 'feel good factor', where electors are content with their income, levels of taxation and the services provided for them, is important for those wishing to retain power. However, voters who feel that none of the mainstream political parties represents them are unlikely to vote, and in the 2005 general election only 60% of British voters actually voted; only 9.5 million out of an electorate of 44 million voted for the winning party.

The feel-good factor can easily be upset by economic depression, shortages of key resources like food or fuel, excessive taxation, low income levels, inflation and unemployment and by disquieting factors such as war, terrorism or environmental disaster.

Newspapers concentrate on negative or positive aspects of life in accordance with their own political allegiances and overall philosophy, and their behaviour has an important influence on the 'feel good factor'.

EXAMINER'S TIP

Remember that television news and current affairs programmes have an obligation to offer balanced accounts of political events, particularly at election times, and can be reported to Ofcom if they are not impartial. Newspapers have no such obligation and are much more biased politically; they are bound only by libel laws and by referral to the Press Complaints Commission.

British quality daily newspapers

These are directed at a readership of predominantly A, B and C1 social class brackets and are characterised by an emphasis on hard political, economic and world news, with less emphasis on sensationalism. All circulation figures given below are based on 'average net circulation'. They are produced by the Audit of Circulation.

The Times
- Ownership: News International (a division of The News Corporation); Chairman: Rupert Murdoch
- Politics: centre right, with qualified support for New Labour
- Circulation: 675,030 (October 2006)

The Times followed the *Independent* with its relaunch in compact (tabloid) format in 2004. Its accessible style and flexible politics help secure its market position as the leading challenger to the *Daily Telegraph*.

The Independent
- Ownership: Independent News and Media
- Politics: centre, with an independent voice
- Circulation: 254,854 (October 2006)

Having successfully led the compact (tabloid) revolution among the quality dailies, and increased its authority as an independent voice with its relentless criticism of the war in Iraq, the *Independent* has slightly improved its circulation in a difficult market. It is distinguished on the newsstand by its use of single-issue front page spreads.

The Guardian
- Ownership: Guardian Media Group
- Politics: centre left, with qualified support for New Labour
- Circulation: 362,844 (October 2006)

With a successfully achieved 'Berliner' relaunch (slightly larger than tabloid format) in the autumn of 2005, the *Guardian* has a secure position on the centre left, with a solid, young readership base.

The Daily Telegraph
- Ownership: the Barclay brothers
- Politics: right wing, with support for the Conservative Party
- Circulation: 898,289 (October 2006)

Having been through a difficult period involving a disputed change of ownership, with its former owner (Lord) Conrad Black facing charges for misuse of funds from his own company, the *Daily Telegraph* was relaunched in late 2005. With its traditional appearance (and with critics suggesting there were few obvious signs of change, other than the paper seeming more like the *Daily Mail*), its future direction still seems uncertain.

The Financial Times
- Ownership: Pearson
- Politics: centre
- Circulation: 416,367 (October 2006)

This distinctive pink broadsheet newspaper is required reading for the business community and is developing international editions. It provides informed, objective commentary on economic and business affairs with a global perspective and takes a non-partisan position in relation to British politics.

A note on format: former quality broadsheet newspapers *The Times*, the *Independent* and the *Guardian* are now published in Compact or Berliner formats. The *Daily Telegraph* and *Financial Times* retain their traditional broadsheet newsprint size.

British quality Sunday newspapers
The Sunday Times
- Ownership: News International (a division of The News Corporation); Chairman: Rupert Murdoch
- Politics: centre right, with support for New Labour
- Circulation: 1,354,489 (October 2006)

This is the market leader for the Sunday qualities; with flexible politics, the paper seems to have its position assured. Marketed as '*the* Sunday papers', its bulk and comprehensive coverage of the Sunday scene make it the obvious quality choice for many, in spite of its subtle bias towards News International interests.

Independent on Sunday
- Ownership: Independent News and Media
- Politics: centre, with no clear political allegiance
- Circulation: 218,240 (October 2006)

This paper pioneered the new compact format. Together with its sister paper the *Independent*, it took a strongly anti-government line on the invasion of Iraq and increased circulation as a result.

The Observer
- Ownership: the Guardian Media Group
- Politics: centre left, supporting New Labour
- Circulation: 439,892 (October 2006)

Following its sister paper the *Guardian*, it adopted a Berliner format in early 2006. Its support for the Iraq invasion caused problems for some of the paper's readership, who found a new home with the *Independent on Sunday*. The *Observer* is happiest in its defence of civil liberties and its columnists have taken a strong stand on the perceived authoritarianism of the New Labour government.

The Sunday Telegraph
- Ownership: the Barclay brothers
- Politics: right wing, supporting the Conservative party
- Circulation: 653,664 (October 2006)
- Faced with an ageing and declining readership, and with the same difficulties as its daily sister paper over the wrangle surrounding its ownership and the criminal charges against its former owner, the *Sunday Telegraph* underwent a modest relaunch in 2005.

Tabloid newspapers
These are published in tabloid format (approximately 40 cm × 30 cm), but the term tabloid is also used to describe the kind of popular sensational journalism found in these newspapers. They are categorised as 'popular' or 'red top' tabloids (their mastheads are printed in red): the *Sun,* the *Daily Mirror* and the *Star*; and 'mid-market' or 'black top' tabloids: the *Daily Mail* and the *Daily Express.*

Characteristics
Tabloids are aimed at a readership of C2, D and E social class brackets. They are characterised by large headlines written in exaggerated, often alliterative, monosyllabic phrases, which accompany sensational or dramatic photographs.

Front pages are usually based on a single issue, covering just one story, and involve celebrities or other sensational storylines rather than current political issues and debates.

Overall contents of 'popular' tabloids are based on an entertainment agenda, with emphasis on celebrity, television, sex, sport, scandal and sensation (see below), and with very limited foreign news coverage unless British interests are directly affected.

The *Daily Mail* has more serious journalistic content, longer features and more hard news.

Tabloid language
The language used by tabloid newspapers is designed to grab the reader's attention and engage in an informal one-way conversation. It is **subjective** — adopting a point of view on behalf of the reader — and assumes the reader's agreement with the position adopted by the newspaper.

Tabloids use a range of rhetorical literary devices for this purpose. These include:
- **alliteration:** often used in headlines to grab attention and create memorable phrases, for example 'Big BBC bung for Brucie' (the *Sun* on the BBC's contract money for Bruce Forsythe) and 'Tone your tummy' (keep fit advice)
- **rhyme:** 'Kate shuts the gate' (the *Sun*, 22 April 2006)
- **metaphor:** 'Lions maul Russian bear' (England versus Russia soccer match)
- **puns:** 'That's a fat lotto good' (the *Sun*, 22 April 2006, on lottery cash for the already wealthy Manchester United)
- **hyperbole:** 'England massacred, fans gutted!'

Another feature of the language is the casual familiarity created by the use of:

- **slang and popular idiom:** 'hubby', 'babe', 'wasted', 'bender', 'cheater', 'boobs', 'footie', 'dosh', 'gutted'
- **misspelled words:** 'It's the Sun wot won it!' *(1992 general election);* 'Gotcha!' (on the sinking of the Argentine cruiser *General Belgrano* during the Falklands War in 1982)
- **clichés:** 'I was over the moon'

Tabloid news agendas

Tabloid newspapers cover many political stories, but their overall news agenda is likely to be based on the following areas:

- public and private morality — financial affairs, sexual behaviour and relationships of those in the public eye
- perceived threats to the wellbeing of the community, whether physical, economic, cultural or social; this means emphasis on crime and punishment, taxation, income and expenditure levels, issues involving asylum and immigration, and 'moral panic' issues involving paedophilia, threats to children, the family and traditional values
- crime and punishment — court reports with sensational treatment
- sport — particularly football — and the careers of sporting heroes
- human interest stories involving individual triumphs and tragedies, illness and recovery, loss of loved ones, and individual acts of bravery and courage; this area also includes ordinary individuals as victims of bureaucracies, or the failings of government, the police or institutions such as the National Health Service
- health, beauty and diet-related subject matter directed at female readers
- the following of television soap agendas and the lives of the stars and celebrities
- National lottery, competitions, prizes and other transformational processes that offer escapism to readers
- glamour and fashion in all titles and glamour as soft pornography in the *Sun* and the *Star*

Moral panic

Stan Cohen first used this term in his book *Folk Devils and Moral Panics* (1972), which considered the media reaction to violent confrontations between Mods and Rockers during the 1960s. It is used to explain the way in which the focus by the media on the behaviour of a social group or an event can be inflated by sensational reporting, and how the repeated use of stereotypes can result in a public overreaction or panic at a perceived threat to society. The key element is the feeling that the situation is out of control in some way and therefore represents a threat to the moral order.

Classic moral panics

- **1960s:** Mods and Rockers fighting in the streets (fear of breakdown of law and order, with youth out of control)
- **1970s:** the *Oz* magazine *School Kids Edition* (1970 (fear of pornography and subversive material corrupting the young, even when in this case the magazine was produced by the young themselves)
- **1970s–1980s:** *The Exorcist* caused controversy at the cinema and was banned on video for 15 years (fear that blasphemy and Satanism could lead to the undermining of moral values)
- **1980s:** video nasties — some videos regarded as offensive by the film censors were banned, including *I Spit on Your Grave, Driller Killer* and *The Texas Chainsaw Massacre* (fear that viewing leads to uncontrolled copycat violence and moral degeneracy)

- **1990s:** murder of Jamie Bulger, and suggested link with film *Child's Play 3* (fear that watching videos leads to copycat crime including murder)
- **2000s:** rap music and other alternative music lyrics (fear that lyrics could encourage gun crime)

In other recent moral panics, it was reported that Marilyn Manson songs listened to by impressionable young men led them to commit the Columbine High School massacre. Lyrics concerning gun crime, sexual violence and drug abuse have been accused of endorsing and encouraging antisocial and criminal behaviour. The garage band So Solid Crew was accused by government minister Kim Howells of glorifying violence after two girls were shot dead in Birmingham in a drive-by gang shooting on New Year's Eve, 2002.

Tabloid daily newspapers
The Daily Mail
- Ownership: Associated Newspapers
- Politics: right of centre, supporting the Conservative Party
- Circulation: 2,381,461 (October 2006)

The *Daily Mail* is the bastion of 'middle England', the solid conservative-voting middle class. It is described as a 'black top' (its masthead is in black rather than red ink) to distinguish it from the more 'downmarket' red tops like the *Sun*, the *Mirror* and the *Star*.

During the 1980s, under the editorship of David English, it was the favourite newspaper of the Prime Minister Margaret Thatcher, who saw it as representing both her own views and the views of her supporters.

Faced with a long period in power for New Labour, the paper has consolidated its position and increased its circulation, offering both qualified support and criticism of the government, depending on the issues.

The Daily Express
- Ownership: Northern and Shell (Richard Desmond)
- Politics: right of centre, mid-market, mixed politics
- Circulation: 829,504 (October 2006)

Formerly a rival to the *Daily Mail*, the *Express* is now overshadowed by the more successful paper, and its future is influenced by the wider media interests of its owner, Richard Desmond.

The Daily Star
- Ownership: Northern and Shell (Richard Desmond)
- Politics: vague populism
- Circulation: 828,728 (October 2006)

Originally launched in 1978 as a lads' newspaper, it has increased sales modestly with a diet of cheerful soap and celebrity gossip, a touch of sleaze, some football and a general indifference to world affairs, which appeals to those seeking escape from depressing hard news realities.

The Sun
- Ownership: News International (the News Corporation)
- Politics: currently New Labour, but flexible
- Circulation: 3,223,841 (October 2006)

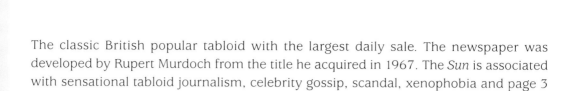

The classic British popular tabloid with the largest daily sale. The newspaper was developed by Rupert Murdoch from the title he acquired in 1967. The *Sun* is associated with sensational tabloid journalism, celebrity gossip, scandal, xenophobia and page 3 girls.

The newspaper claims to have affected the outcome of British general elections since the early 1970s, and in 1997 it switched its support from the Conservatives to New Labour.

Although its circulation has fallen in recent years along with that of its rival the *Daily Mirror*, the government is still concerned to retain the support of *Sun* readers, as this is seen as crucial for securing election victories. For instance, government ministers use interviews with the *Sun* as a means of addressing readers on important issues, while the *Sun's* strong opposition to the euro is seen as a factor in the New Labour government's reluctance to test public opinion on whether or not to join the European currency.

It appointed the first female editor of a national tabloid, Rebekah Wade, in January 2003.

The Daily Mirror

- Ownership: Trinity Mirror
- Politics: New Labour, popular
- Circulation: 1,662,930 (October 2006)

Formerly a powerful supporter of the traditional Labour Party from the late 1930s, the *Daily Mirror* lost both readership and influence when faced with intensive competition for its readership from the *Sun* during the late 1960s.

Having survived a disastrous period under the ownership of corrupt tycoon Robert Maxwell in the 1980s and early 1990s, it has achieved a more secure position with its current owners.

Its editorial policy was a source of controversy during the Iraq war when it refused to back British intervention; after arguments with the newspaper's publishers in 2004 over fake photographs purporting to show Iraqi prisoners being brutalised by British soldiers, the editor Piers Morgan was sacked.

Tabloid Sunday newspapers

The Mail on Sunday

- Ownership: Associated Newspapers
- Politics: right of centre, mid-market
- Circulation: 2,285,632 (October 2006)

This was successfully launched as the Sunday version of the *Daily Mail*, with all the characteristics of its daily partner.

The Sunday Express

- Ownership: Northern and Shell (Richard Desmond)
- Politics: right of centre, mid-market
- Circulation: 826,730 (October 2006)

Like its weekday sister paper, the *Sunday Express* runs far behind its much stronger rival, the *Mail on Sunday*.

The News of the World
- Ownership: News International (the News Corporation)
- Politics: broadly New Labour, popular
- Circulation: 3,538,886 (October 2006)

This paper has the largest circulation of any newspaper. It is regarded as sensational, with its focus on sex, sleaze, celebrity and scandal.

The Sunday Mirror
- Ownership: Trinity Mirror
- Politics: left of centre, New Labour, popular
- Circulation:1,463,970 (October 2006)

This has much the same values and agenda as the *Daily Mirror*.

The People
- Ownership: Trinity Mirror
- Politics: New Labour, popular
- Circulation: 859,908 (October 2006)

At one time a distinctive paper with a reputation for strong left wing journalism and comment, the *People* is now virtually indistinguishable from its stable mate the *Sunday Mirror*.

Regional newspapers
These include the following:
- London area: *Evening Standard* (Associated Newspapers)
- Birmingham area: *Birmingham Post*, *Evening Mail* (Trinity Mirror)
- Manchester area: *Manchester Evening News* (Guardian Media Group)
- Yorkshire: *Yorkshire Post* (Johnston Press)
- Northeast: *Newcastle Evening Chronicle* (Trinity Mirror)
- Scotland: *The Scotsman* (Johnston Press)
- Southwest: *Bristol Evening Post* (Associated Newspapers); *Western Morning News* (Associated Newspapers)

Application of key concepts to the study of regional newspapers
- What is their news agenda?
- What methods are used to attract readers?
- How do they differ from the national press?
- How does their advertising content differ from national papers?

Genre
- Usually tabloid format
- Attention-grabbing headlines
- A large proportion of photos

Representation
- Local people and places
- Local government
- Local services
- Mainstream values

Audience
- Regionally defined
- Family focused
- Local/narrow cast — not read outside the area
- No socioeconomic class distinction, as seen in the national press

Values and ideology
- Mainstream — part of the community
- Local politics and issues, such as the closure of local hospitals; other popular issues include road safety, education, local crime and policing policies, social services, court reports, and the activities of local celebrities
- Local councillors and MPs rather than a national agenda
- Local angles on national stories — for example, 'Gulf war hero's return to proud mum'

Institution
- Multi-ownership — many titles owned by one company; Associated Newspapers, Trinity Mirror and Johnston Press are major players across the country
- Cross-media ownership — *Manchester Evening News* is part of the Guardian Media Group and the London *Evening Standard* is owned by Associated Newspapers
- Free delivery and a free version of the paper are options in target areas
- Links with local radio

Language and content
- Usually tabloid rather than quality
- Contents subject to press releases from interested groups, such as the police and local schools
- Campaigning from local pressure groups — for example, 'Save our playing fields from development!'
- Local weather
- Local advertising
- Strong emphasis on local sport
- Local focus on travel/gossip/television/entertainment
- Notice board for local jobs, services, lonely hearts, buy-and-sell columns etc.

Advertising
- Advertising often has local 'spin' on national campaigns, such as the regional opening of a national store
- Local restaurants and entertainments
- Inclusion of local fliers
- High proportion of adverts — often difficult to distinguish from real journalism
- Importance of local property and car ads

Point for discussion

In a multicultural environment, will ethnically or culturally targeted newspapers become increasingly important? *The Voice* (published by Voice Communications Group and founded in 1982) is targeted at young black Britons with the aim of positive representation of black interests and fighting for fairness and equality. Its circulation is modest at fewer than 50,000 copies and there is now strong competition from ethnically focused local radio stations.

TERMINOLOGY

Banner: a strip telling the reader what is in the paper — usually at top of the page

Black-on-tone: black type on a toned background

Brief: a few lines summarising the article in the paper

By-line: the name of the journalist who wrote the article

Caption: the phrase that explains, interprets and anchors the photograph

Cropping: the practice of cutting and trimming photographs in newspapers and magazines, either to fit available space or to alter or emphasise elements of the image

Cross head: the heading of a subsection printed within the body of the article

Drop-cap: a large capital letter at the beginning of the article which drops into the surrounding text

Half lead story: the second story

Headline: a memorable phrase to attract attention

Lead story: the main story

Masthead: the name or title of the newspaper

Photograph: this accompanies articles or acts as the key focus of a front page; sometimes the photograph *is* the story

Plug: a free mention of a service or product

Strapline: a memorable phrase or slogan associated with the masthead and what the paper stands for

This chapter is largely concerned with AQA A2 Unit 4, but page 84 has a brief note on the OCR AS Unit 2732 case study.

1 Specification focus: AQA Unit 4 (A2)

This unit consists of four sections, each with a choice of two questions. You will be required to answer two questions taken from any two sections. These will usually be the sections you have prepared for in your centre and you are not advised to tackle questions from sections you have not covered during your course.

The sections are:
- The production and manufacture of news
- Representations
- Genre
- Media audiences

These are dealt with in turn below.

1.1 The production and manufacture of news
News sources
News agencies
Examples include Associated Press, Agence France Press and Reuters. These organisations specialise in the collection and dissemination of news stories worldwide. Associated Press is the largest and oldest global agency. It was founded in 1848 and has 3700 employees, 240 bureaus, an online news service, a television news service and a 24-hour radio service.

Journalists and their contacts
Journalists are proactive in seeking out news stories and pursuing their own specialist interests. For example, BBC journalist Michael Crick is well known for pursuing politicians in search of scandal in both their public and private affairs.

Press releases
These are circulated by organisations and companies as a means of publicising and explaining their activities or in response to criticism. They are prepared by press officers or communications officers on behalf of the company and represent only the company's version of events.

Emergency services
These services provide sources of news relating to crime, road accidents, fires and other events.

Courts
Court reporters provide accounts of court proceedings and the sentences handed out to convicted offenders.

Members of the public
Anyone can be a source of news as an eyewitness, particularly with the advent of mobile phones and camera phones. The camera phones of tube passengers on 7 July 2005 provided graphic images of the scenes inside the bombed trains after the London terrorist attacks.

Corporate news machines

Examples include CNN, BBC 24, Fox and Sky. These global news machines have their own newsgathering staff throughout the world.

Ideology

All news is constructed within an ideological framework.

Bias, 'spin' and propaganda

Even though news organisations may claim to be objective in the coverage of events, the nature of news makes true objectivity difficult to achieve for the following reasons:

- Control of the news agenda is important to politicians who employ 'spin doctors' and communications managers to direct news dissemination and challenge versions of events that conflict with the party's policies.
- News is selective; not all events are reported, so it is impossible for news to present a totally objective picture of the world.
- News is institutional, as it is produced by organisations that have their own values and ideology, which affect news selection and presentation.
- News is culturally determined; it is produced within a cultural framework of attitudes, beliefs and values. For example, CNN news is different from al-Jazeera.
- News is interpreted by reporters and editors who make value judgements on what is being shown and discussed.
- News is directed at a target audience and adapted to suit the assumed perspectives of that audience. For example, the *Guardian* does not have the same news agenda as the *Sun*.
- News is increasingly seen as **dumbed down** entertainment, and the need to attract and maintain an audience can take priority over balance and objectivity. For example, the BBC Six O'Clock news on 5 April 2006 gave 15 seconds to industrial and student unrest in France involving one million demonstrators and strikers and which was seen as a threat to the survival of the French government, and followed this up with 2 minutes of interviews with English travellers delayed at airports as a result. This demonstrates the tabloid value: serious news in western Europe is only of interest if it affects British people.

Examples of conflict between politicians and journalists

- During the Vietnam War, journalists who had free access to the conflict and who filed many negative reports and photographs were accused of undermining the US war effort and encouraging the antiwar movement.
- During the Falklands conflict of 1982, the BBC was criticised by the British government for taking an impartial view of military events rather than supporting the government line.
- During the first Gulf War in 1991, the US army provided detailed daily briefings of the conflict for television news channels to reassure audiences at home that the conflict was both measured and well managed, with minimal casualties. **Embedded journalists** were controlled by the military and could report only what was shown to them. The realities of huge Iraqi casualties including civilians emerged only towards the end of the conflict.
- Following the controversial decision by the British government to join the USA in the invasion of Iraq in 2003, the BBC was involved in a protracted row over its attempts to challenge government justification for the war. The row ended with the resignation of Greg Dyke as Director General of the BBC and the departure of Alistair Campbell

as the government's Communications Manager. The dispute highlighted the delicate relationship between an elected government and the BBC. The government is responsible for the periodic renewal of the BBC's charter and is influential in BBC appointments, while the BBC is keen to demonstrate its resistance to government interference in editorial decisions.

- The Arab television news channel al-Jazeera's reporting of the invasion of Iraq from an Arab perspective so annoyed the Americans that journalists and one of the channel's offices were targeted by US forces. It was suggested that the US forces considered bombing the television station. If al-Jazeera were not broadcasting in the Middle East then only the western version of events would be screened.

TERMINOLOGY

Bias: the ideological slanting of a media text to represent one point of view more favourably than another.

Embedded journalist: a journalist operating alongside a military unit in a combat zone and subject to military control and restrictions. An embedded journalist runs the risk of appearing to be a mouthpiece for the military authorities.

Propaganda: the deliberate distortion of representations by the selection of images and storylines in such a way as to advance a particular ideology or point of view at the expense of all others. Propaganda uses lies, half truths and deception and is designed to persuade an audience to accept the viewpoint being offered.

Spin: manipulated information offered to journalists by press officers and communication managers (sometimes called 'spin doctors'), whose aim is to ensure that their employers are favourably represented.

News values

This term is used by researchers to describe the various criteria involved in the selection of news by broadcasters and journalists. It is often associated with the researchers Galtung and Ruge but has been adapted and expanded by other analysts. The following is a comprehensive list:

- **frequency** — news needs to happen on a daily and frequent basis to meet schedules
- **cultural proximity** — news needs to be close to home or related to home issues
- **threshold** — news needs to be of sufficient importance to attract attention; big events get noticed more than small ones
- **negativity** — bad news has priority over good news
- **predictability** — news tends to anticipate and justify expected outcomes
- **unexpectedness** — news needs to seem unexpected, even though most of it takes place within predictable patterns
- **continuity** — following up a big story is seen as newsworthy
- **unambiguity** — events with a clear meaning are more likely to be reported than complex issues
- **composition** — news is subject to editorial constructions and reflects individual editorial choices, the constraints of the medium and organisational values
- **personalisation** — events that can be made personal get priority
- **reference to elite nations** — powerful nations (usually Western) have priority coverage
- **reference to elite people** — celebrities get more coverage than unknown people
- **narrativisation** — news is constructed as a story and all elements of narrative theory apply

- **visual imperative** — television news and tabloid journalism tend to be driven by pictures and what is available

Agenda setting

Agenda setting refers to the ability of all news media to decide in what order and with what emphasis they choose to report on events.

- Newspapers and news broadcasts (possibly in line with some of the news values identified above) concentrate on some events rather than others.
- An audience's perception of the importance and significance of events can be shown to be in direct proportion to the amount of media coverage the events receive. Events that receive no coverage provoke no audience response, as the audience remains ignorant of the fact that they have taken place.
- The practice of agenda setting can be illustrated by a review of the front pages of daily newspapers published on the same day; a wide range of different topics is usually to be seen.
- The term 'agenda setting' implies that, in rank order, items at the top of the agenda will be seen as more important than those at the bottom.

The struggle to set and control the news agenda is an important part of a political party's strategy at election time and a government's overall strategy when in office. 'Spin doctors' seek to direct the news media's attention into areas where the parties feel comfortable and away from areas where they are embarrassed or vulnerable. Bad news — such as an increase in taxation or high unemployment figures — will often be released by government departments when other issues dominate the news, in the hope that they will receive less attention or not be noticed at all. Jo Moore, a government communications officer, famously said in a memorandum to staff that the events of 9/11 made it a good day to bury bad news. By contrast, when there seems little of importance on the news agenda, items that would otherwise receive no coverage at all find their way to the top and the public's perception of their importance is greatly increased.

News and new technologies

Technological developments have made news more immediate and accessible.

More immediate

News reports are instantly flashed around the world and satellite phone technology allows instant communication with journalists, even in the remotest areas. The concept of 'breaking news' and the crawler text at the bottom of news channel reports emphasises the continuing process of news gathering and reporting.

More accessible

News is available on 24-hour dedicated channels such as Sky, CNN and BBC News 24, and also on the internet and mobile phones, in addition to traditional television and radio bulletins. Interaction and selection is made possible through the use of the digital red button, which allows viewers to access the news in a split screen format, choose the headlines they want expanded and revisit a topic at will.

News presentation

News presentation has become increasingly informal on **mainstream** television channels, as a means of engaging and holding an audience. News is seen as entertainment and the object is to hold on to the audience by promising excitement to come throughout the bulletin.

Dedicated news channels such as Sky News and BBC News 24 are more tr͏
formal in their studio presentation, with a 'crawler' line of breaking r͏
the bottom of the screen and formal presentations by newsreaders͏
usually across a desk. The reasons for this are:

- viewers have selected the news channels because they are a niche audience already interested in the news rather than being part of a general audience for an evening's viewing, as is the case with a terrestrial channel's mainstream bulletins
- a dedicated niche audience means there is not the same commercial need for **dumbing down** in order to grab and hold the viewers' attention

Presentation is also affected by the choice of digital options for interaction, with the use of split screens and headline menus for audiences to choose from.

Characteristics of mainstream news bulletins

- Mainstream news programmes such as the BBC's *News at Ten* and ITV1's *News at 10.30* are breaks in evening programming and need to a have a magazine style of presentation to retain the channel's viewers.
- BBC1 and ITV1 bulletins have regional dimensions but retain the role of 'anchor man/woman' in the studio.
- Presentation can now be less formal than before, with *Five News* being the first to introduce a presenter (Kirsty Young) sitting on the desk rather than behind it.
- *Channel 4 News* is an in-depth, hour-long news programme scheduled at 7 p.m. so that it does not to break up mid-evening viewing. It has attracted a dedicated audience for its particular blend of journalism and comment. Its *More 4* digital option allows interaction between the anchorman Jon Snow and the audience via 'Snowmail'.
- BBC2's *Newsnight* has an in-depth approach to selected topics drawn from the news agenda of the day, combined with short news summaries and arts coverage. Its use of CGI to construct 'virtual' sets to provide context for the narrative reports and the relaxed set with sofas and atmospheric lighting give the programme a distinctive character but have not attracted a larger audience.

TERMINOLOGY

Dumbing down: the practice of reducing the intellectual or academic content of a media text in order to increase its entertainment value and make it accessible to a larger audience.

Mainstream: a term describing the dominant cultural values of the majority of the population.

1.2 Representations

Social groups

Those commonly studied for AS and A2 include:

- ethnic minorities
- gays and lesbians
- gender: men/women, masculinity/femininity
- teenagers
- the disabled
- asylum seekers

Positive and negative representations

Positive representations portray a group in ways of which the group would approve and which emphasise its positive contributions to a society.

Negative representations are associated with stereotypical or prejudiced portrayals that emphasise negative or unflattering features of the group, often presenting it as a threat or burden on society.

Question and answer

Q: *Can representations ever present a totally accurate picture of the world?*

A: No. Quite simply, representations are only selective and partial versions of the real and are always subject to the process of mediation whereby they are constructed in line with the constraints of the medium used and the attitudes, beliefs and values of those involved in the creation of the media product.

Issues of representation

Ethic minorities

- Racism and the representation of racial stereotypes have been identified particularly by the work of Stuart Hall (1995), who argued that in period films black people were traditionally represented as entertainers, faithful slaves or happy natives.
- Texts as background: *Shaft* (Gordon Parks 1971), *Baby Father* (BBC TV 2003), *Bend it Like Beckham* (Gurinder Chadha 2002) and *Bhaji on the Beach* (Gurinder Chadha 2000).

Gays and lesbians

- The representation of homosexuality as an illegal activity was masked and stereotyped with the use of camp character traits and innuendo until its legalisation in 1967. Relationships were often hinted at rather than openly expressed and the gay characters were frequently presented as being emotionally disturbed or depraved. An example is *The Servant* (Joseph Losey 1963, screenplay Harold Pinter). Homosexuality was often a source of blackmail and associated with illegal behaviour and criminality.
- Contemporary representations include *Tipping the Velvet* (BBC2 2002) and *Queer as Folk* (Channel 4 1999).
- Comic representations, such as Daffyd ('the only gay in the village') in *Little Britain* (2004), have moved on from the camp Mr Humphries in the 1970s situation comedy *Are You Being Served?*

Gender

- During the growth of the feminist movement in the 1970s, the representation of women and girls was seen by feminists as often sexually exploitative, negative and reinforcing traditional male stereotypes and patriarchal society. Issues included page 3 models in the *Sun*, perfume advertisements showing naked or alluring women, the '**male gaze**' in film (see Point for discussion, p. 69) and the use of women in passive domestic settings in advertisements, cooking the dinner for their husbands, cleaning the house and trying to look glamorous when he arrives home.
- Although many of the above issues still apply, contemporary representations of women in the post-feminist era have been transformed and many women are now represented in a whole range of roles involving responsibility and power.
- Representation of men has become more of an issue in a post-feminist environment, and issues have arisen where men have been represented as dominated or humiliated by women in advertisements, often for domestic products. Defenders of these representations argue that they are intended to be humorous and produced in a context where male participation in domestic chores is still the exception rather than the rule.

- The 'new man' — more sensitive and caring and less macho — has been a feature of advertising since the late 1980s. Some argue that the 'feminisation' of men in advertising images and in lifestyle marketing of clothes and perfumes is a challenge to traditional masculinity.
- 'New ladism' associated with magazines such as *FHM*, *Maxim* and *Loaded* is seen as a reaction to dominant female representations and the emphasis on 'girl power' by groups such as the Spice Girls in the mid-1990s.

Texts as background

Brief Encounter (David Lean 1946)

Fight Club (David Fincher 1999)

Erin Brockovich (Steven Soderbergh 2000)

Kill Bill Vol. 1 and *Vol. 2* (Quentin Tarantino 2004/5)

Tomb Raider (Simon West 2001)

The Commander (ITV 2005)

Prime Suspect (television; David Drury 1991 onwards)

Point for discussion

Laura Mulvey's theory of 'male gaze' derived from her essay *Visual Pleasure and Narrative Cinema* in 1975, which has been extremely influential in debates concerning the representation of women. Mulvey argued that the film camera takes the male perspective and views the world through male eyes. Women are objects of desire to be possessed or controlled and are seen as such by the camera, assumes a male audience. Mulvey's theory implies that sexist attitudes are reinforced by representations and camera techniques that confirm male dominance.

In over 30 years since Mulvey's essay appeared, there have been great changes in the representation of women and in the 'gaze' of the camera. It is now appropriate to talk of 'female gaze', where male actors are viewed as sex objects for the gratification of women, and this approach can also be applied to television and in particular to advertisements. Look for examples and ask yourself whether male or female 'gaze' applies, or in fact whether the camera's gaze is neutral.

Teenagers

The concept of the teenager was largely invented by advertising and marketing companies in the late 1940s as it became clear, particularly in the USA, that youths involved in the Second World War were not going to settle back into quiet suburban or country life. The popular jive and bebop music styles of the war years and the recognition that teenagers were a separate and increasingly financially independent social group made the direction of products towards them worthwhile. At the same time, the unwillingness of teenagers to settle into traditional adult life in a restless and changing world became a focus of social and political concern. The term 'juvenile delinquent' was devised to describe the rebel generation and a range of film representations created folk heroes out of Marlon Brando in *A Streetcar Named Desire* (Elia Kazan 1951), *The Wild One* and *On the Waterfront* (both Elia Kazan 1954), and James Dean in *East of Eden* (Elia Kazan 1955) and *Rebel Without a Cause* (Nicholas Ray 1955). Dean's early death in a road accident turned him into a youth icon overnight.

1960s representations of teenagers reflected the pop culture of the time, with films like *The Knack...and How to Get It* and *Help!* (Richard Lester 1965), the latter staring the Beatles. Peter Fonda and Dennis Hopper's film *Easy Rider* (1969) was a 'road movie',

which reflected the hippy alternative search for values and identity in modern America, with the lead characters as naive idealists ultimately destroyed by the prejudiced and hate-filled rednecks.

More recent portrayals of teenagers include:

- Kevin the teenager in *Harry Enfield and Chums* (BBC television 1994)
- Vicky Pollard in *Little Britain* (BBC television 2004), who conforms to stereotypical adult views of dysfunctional, selfish, delinquent and immature teenage behaviour
- *Sweet Sixteen* (Ken Loach 2004), which offers a social realist picture of the conflicts and socioeconomic pressures that lead a young teenager — who means well and is trying to sort out his life — into criminal activity and murder
- *Thirteen* (Catherine Hardwicke 2003), which represents the world as seen by a 13-year-old girl

The disabled

- Tod Browning's *Freaks* (1932) was a compilation of disabled characters presented as circus entertainment. Critics saw the film as perverse and morbid, and negative audience reaction meant that it was a financial disaster for the studio, MGM. The film was banned in Britain.
- There has been a change of attitude since the Second World War, with a recognition of the need to build an inclusive society with disability represented honestly and positively.
- The Disability Discrimination Act 1995 requires that the disabled are treated with respect and inclusion.
- Positive representations of disability are shown in many films: in *Four Weddings and a Funeral* (Mike Newell 1994), Hugh Grant's character Charles's brother, David, is deaf; in *Inside I'm Dancing* (Damien O'Donnell 2004, BBC films), lead character Michael suffers from cerebral palsy and Rory is almost totally disabled; in *Rainman* (Barry Levinson 1989), Dustin Hoffman's character, Raymond Babbitt, suffers from autism; in *Scent of a Woman* (Martin Brest 1993), Al Pacino's character, Frank Slade, is blind.
- Comical representation of faked disability is seen in the Lou and Andy sketches in *Little Britain* (BBC television 2004).

Asylum seekers

This became an issue in the twenty-first century with an increase in the flow of people from Africa, Asia and Eastern Europe seeking work or asylum in western European countries. Negative representation by the British tabloid press helped to create a moral panic concerning the number of asylum seekers and their alleged creation of social disruption and involvement in crime. Treating vulnerable minorities as **scapegoats** is easier then facing up to social problems created by homelessness and unemployment.

Social realist film treatment of the issues — for example *Dirty Pretty Things* (Stephen Frears 2002) — has drawn attention to this area, and there have been short films illustrating the exploitation of asylum seekers by criminal gang masters who employ labourers below the legal rates of pay (e.g. *Job Street*, Matthew Whitecross 2004).

TERMINOLOGY

Scapegoat: a person or group of people blamed by a society for all the problems it faces, and victimised as a result.

Places

Analysing the representation of places involves identifying the location and exploring a range of media representations:

- **New York:** *New York, New York* (Martin Scorsese 1977), *Taxi Driver* (Martin Scorsese 1975), *Wall Street* (Oliver Stone 1987), *Friends* (David Crane 1994–2004)
- **Scotland:** *Taggart* (television crime drama 1983–93), *Rab C. Nesbitt* (BBC2 sitcom 1989–93), *Monarch of the Glen* (BBC television 2000–2005), *Rob Roy* (Michael Caton-Jones 1995), *Braveheart* (Mel Gibson 1995), *Sweet Sixteen* (Ken Loach 2003)
- **London:** *Grange Hill* (children's school soap opera created by Phil Redmond 1978–), *Notting Hill* (Roger Michel 1999), *Dirty Pretty Things* (Stephen Frears 2002), *EastEnders* (BBC television 1985–)
- **Paris:** *Maigret* (John Glenister 1992 — remake of a 1960s television favourite), *La Haine* (Mathieu Kassovitz 1995), *Moulin Rouge* (Baz Luhrmann 2001), *The Dreamers* (Bernardo Bertolucci 2004)
- **Northwest England:** *Coronation Street* (Granada Television 1960–), *Boys from the Blackstuff* (television drama, Alan Bleasdale 1982), *Cold Feet* (Granada Television 1997–2003), *The Royle Family* (BBC 1998), *Shameless* (Channel 4 2005), *Hollyoaks* (Channel 4 1995–)
- **Northeast England:** *Our Friends in the North* (BBC2 1996), *Auf Wiedersehen Pet* (BBC drama 1983), *Stormy Monday* (Mike Figgis 1988)

Point for discusssion

The representation of places is strongly dependent on a range of historical, social, cultural, economic and political assumptions. European capital cities (such as Paris) carry associations reflecting the traditional view of their country of origin.

- Paris is associated with artists and art, cabaret and nightlife, love and romance, good food and famous landmarks. Holiday companies will emphasise traditional aspects of the city in their adverts to make it appealing to customers, as depicted in *Moulin Rouge* (Baz Luhrmann 2001), *French Kiss* (Lawrence Kasdan 1995) and *The Last Time I Saw Paris* (Richard Brooks 1954). They will not draw attention to evidence of social conflict: the high level of homelessness, unrest and racism in the largely immigrant populated suburbs, high levels of youth unemployment, HIV infection and drug abuse — a portrayal seen in *La Haine* (Mathieu Kassovitz 1995).
- Representations of the north of England have traditionally emphasised the working-class lifestyle, with back-to-back housing and close knit family communities, as seen in *Coronation Street* and *The Royle Family* and in the British 'New Wave' classic *A Kind of Loving* (John Schlesinger 1962). *Shameless* (Channel 4 2004–) makes social realist comedy out of family and community breakdown, emphasising the inherent determination and optimism of families of the underclass who live outside the norms of society and make their own rules of behaviour. The comedy genre conceals deeply disturbing social realities on estates in north and south Manchester.

Stereotyping

Stereotyping is the social classification of individuals, groups of people and places by identifying common characteristics and applying them in an oversimplified and generalised way. The classification represents value judgements and assumptions about the individual, group or place concerned.

Questions and answers

Q: Are stereotypes resistant to change?

A: Yes, because once established in people's minds they stay there, as people are unwilling to change their opinions. Research shows that, in general, individuals will seek out information that confirms their existing opinions and reject information that challenges them. This is partly explained in the **theory of cognitive dissonance** developed by Leon Festinger in 1957, which argues that individuals will resist adjusting an attitude or viewpoint unless faced with overwhelming evidence or experience that it is ill-founded. Festinger believes that changing your mind creates 'cognitive dissonance' — a disagreeable state of mental contradiction — and requires a wholesale adjustment of views to restore 'cognitive consistency' or mental harmony. Put simply, having formed a judgement, people like to be proved right and they resist evidence that puts them in the wrong.

Q: Do stereotypes change over time?

A: Yes, eventually, particularly if media representations are used to challenge them. This is why it is so important to represent, for example, racial minorities positively, as integrated, socially equal and financially successful members of society, present in all social levels. The more people are exposed to positive representations of this kind the more they will come to accept them as the norm.

A final point to remember is that stereotypes are, by their nature, crude generalisations used as a form of mental categorisation — the first point of reference in perceiving and assessing individuals, groups and places. The term 'stereotype' carries with it negative connotations and the implicit understanding that a closer and more detailed evaluation of the individual, group or place will result in more accurate assessment. The fact is that nobody really believes that all the French are good cooks, all Italians make good lovers, all Yorkshire men are mean and all blondes are dumb!

Point for discusssion

The representation of nurses in British television is an interesting example of changes in stereotypes.

- Traditional representation is exemplified in the classic ITV series *Emergency Ward 10* (1957–67, with an audience in 1959 of over 12 million). The series tended to romanticise the nursing profession by showing nurses (all women) as professional, dedicated carers, saving lives while seeking romance with higher status male doctors.

- *Angels* (1975–83) was an unglamorous depiction of the profession, showing student nurses facing up to problems of sexual promiscuity, alcoholism and other hard hitting social issues while working in a pressurised NHS. With a multiethnic cast, its aim was authenticity, with actresses required to spend time on a hospital ward to add to the realism of the programme. The title of the series reflected the high public esteem for nursing profession. This treatment was carried through into the BBC's *Casualty* (1986–), with *Holby City* (1999–) as a spin-off.

- By contrast, *No Angels* (Channel 4 2004–) uses comedy drama to show four women balancing a difficult job in today's NHS with complicated personal lives that revolve around sexual promiscuity, single parenthood and personal aspirations.

- The move from *Angels* to *No Angels* suggests a change in attitude and the public's expectations of the profession as a whole

1.3 Genre

A genre is a category of media products that are classed as being similar in form and type.

Genre theory

This is concerned with identifying the characteristics of genres and the relationship between genres, audiences, media texts and media producers. Genres can be used to target specific audience groups with predictable expectations of audience numbers and responses.

Point for discusssion

Richard Dyer is an influential genre theorist who in 1973 argued that genres are pleasurable because they offer escapist fantasies into fictional worlds that remove the boredom and pressures of reality. He sees these worlds as Utopian (i.e. idealised and perfect), offering the audience an escape from everyday problems and routines, together with an abundance of energy, excitement, spontaneity and community, none of which is present in their everyday lives.

Quotations from genre theorists

Genres are agents of ideological closure; they limit the meaning potential of a given text (Hartley). This means that within a classic western film the expected roles and behaviour of stock characters in stock situations limits unexpected developments of the narrative. More recently, genres have been adapted to allow alternative representations, such as in *Dances With Wolves* (Kevin Costner 1990), where Indians are portrayed as 'good' and the cavalry as 'bad', and gay cowboys challenging the macho stereotype in *Brokeback Mountain* (Ang Lee 2005).

Genres are typical forms of texts, which link kinds of producers, consumers, topic, medium, manner and occasion. (Hodge and Kress). An example would be a Disney classic cartoon fairy tale, using computer generated animation, with general release in multiplex cinemas and video and internet availability.

One advantage of genres is that they can rely on readers already having knowledge and expectations about the works within a genre (Fowler). This means that producers do not have to explain the conventions of a text and the nature of characters, as audiences are already familiar with them.

Genres can be seen as a kind of shorthand, increasing the efficiency of communication (Gledhill). This means that because audiences already know what to expect within a genre, it is not necessary to explain all of the details to them, and narratives can therefore be condensed.

Any text requires what is sometimes called 'cultural capital' on the part of its audience to make sense of it. (Allen). Audiences bring their past knowledge and experience of a genre to a particular text and this enables them to understand it.

The assignment of a text to a genre influences how the text is read (Fiske). This means that if you believe a text to be in a particular genre, you will interpret the text in accordance with your expectations of that genre. For example, the ups and downs of relationships in a romantic comedy such as *Bridget Jones's Diary* (Sharon Maguire 2001)

are not taken very seriously, and the audience does not see the mistakes and failures as tragic, as they expect a happy ending.

Genre constrains the possible ways in which a text is interpreted, guiding readers towards a preferred reading (Fiske). This means that, for example, with a romantic comedy we do not take the behaviour of the characters very seriously as we know that everything will turn out for the best.

Genre may offer various emotional pleasures such as empathy and escapism (Knight). We enjoy identifying with characters and imagining ourselves living their experiences.

Pleasure is derived from repetition and difference (Neale). We like to feel secure with the familiarity of a genre but we also enjoy a surprise.

We derive pleasure from observing how the conventions of a genre are manipulated (Abercrombie). Knowing what to expect makes us enjoy the unexpected.

Enduring genres reflect universal dilemmas and moral conflicts and also appeal to deep psychological needs (Konigsberg). Human experience is repeated in every generation, with the essential dilemmas of life remaining the same — questions of human origins, life, death and the hereafter, the search for love and personal fulfilment, relationships and the family, economic survival, questions of values and religion, war and conflict and the disruption they cause, happiness and tragedy, and fear of the unknown.

Pastiche and parody in genre
- A **pastiche** is a media text made up of pieces of other texts or an imitation of other styles.
- A **parody** is an imitation of one media text by another for comic effect.

Pastiche can involve homage — when one text deliberately imitates the characteristics of another in recognition of that text's importance. *What Lies Beneath (*Robert Zemeckis 2000) contains elements of homage to Alfred Hitchcock's *Psycho* (1960), *Shaun of the Dead* (Edgar Wright 2004) is a parody of *Dawn of the Dead (*George Romero 1978), and *Scary Movie* (Keenan Ivory Wayans 2000) is a parody of slasher horror movies.

Hybrid genres/cross genres
These are a cross between one genre and another, such as *From Dusk till Dawn* (Robert Rodriguez 1992), which starts as a crime drama and becomes a vampire movie. *The Matrix* (Wachowski brothers 1999) is a cross between an action movie and sci-fi, and the *Blade* series (Stephen Norrington 1998) is a cross between action and vampire horror.

Genre and producers
Producers like genres because:
- they are constructed for a known audience with predictable responses
- they use repeated storylines and stock characters
- they allow reuse of sets, props and actors, with consequent financial savings
- they are tried and tested and provide an element of security for investors
- budgets and financial returns are easier to predict
- they allow for clear product and audience differentiation and market segmentation

Genre and audience
An audience likes genres because:
- it knows what to expect
- it can plan viewing with certain expectations

- it enjoys subtle variations within a predictable framework
- it finds genres a consistent form of release and escapism
- it can engage quickly with easily recognisable plots and characters
- it can enjoy predicting outcomes
- it can easily follow the narratives within genres, requiring only a short attention span
- it experiences a sense of cultural and emotional security
- it finds the choice of entertainment easy

Questions and answers

Q: Why do genres develop?

A: Because audiences eventually tire of repetition. Genres are subject to changes in social attitudes, beliefs and values and have to reflect these changing social expectations.

Q: Are genres too predictable and unimaginative?

A: Genres try to avoid this for the following reasons:

- If genres do become too predictable and unimaginative, then audiences decline and investing institutions lose money. Genres have to adapt to reflect changes in social and cultural attitudes, values and expectations.
- Stale genres can be revived by being less predictable and more imaginative. For example, although the western is generally out of favour for its limited mise-en-scène, iconography and narrative potential, *Brokeback Mountain* (Ang Lee 2005), with its theme of homosexuality, has been a great success and reflects current attitudes towards gay relationships.
- The underlying narrative structures of predictable genres like a western can be present in films of different genres — for example, the narrative of *Black Hawk Down* (Ridley Scott 2000) involves sending US air 'cavalry' into hostile territory controlled by 'savages', where they suffer a serious military setback and are pinned down in enemy territory. This triggers a heroic self-sacrificing rescue attempt to 'leave no man behind', which fits easily into a classic US cavalry western genre movie like *She Wore a Yellow Ribbon* (John Ford 1949).
- Audiences seek familiarity and difference within genres and therefore welcome a degree of predictability. The loose conventions give an easy point of reference and allow film makers to take shortcuts by using stock characters and locations that are easily recognisable to the audience, thus requiring little development.
- On the other hand, audiences want plot twists, variations and hybrid developments to keep them interested and retain an enigmatic element in the narrative.
- Films in the twenty-first century are increasingly flexible and unpredictable in terms of genre, mixing elements of several genres to appeal to a wider audience range and to retain audience interest.

Example of a classic film genre: gangster

A gangster genre film is based around the activities of a criminal gang or gangs. Classic gangster movies represent the conflict between good and evil, played out in the slums of the big American cities. The poor, city-dwelling cinema-goers of the early twentieth century could relate to the aspirational dreams of gangsters, who were faced with the legitimate desire to achieve the 'American dream' of wealth and happiness by means of the illegitimate use of crime. As a result, gangster films are usually morally ambivalent.

- The first identifiable gangster film, *The Musketeers of Pig Alley* (D. W. Griffiths 1912) was based on gangs in New York and tackled themes of poverty, crime and retribution.
- *Regeneration* (Raoul Walsh 1915) followed the rise to gangster status of Irish-American immigrants from the slums.
- Representations of gangsters as 'folk heroes' troubled the Hays Office (the US film industry censorship body of the time), and after 1934, studios were forced to make moral pronouncements condemning the behaviour of the gangsters featured in the films. These statements were even backdated to earlier films, such as *The Public Enemy* (William Wellman 1931).
- Gangsters remained folk heroes, in spite of attempts to portray the pursuers as saviours of society. This can be seen in *The G Men* (William Keighley 1935).
- The gangster genre is adaptable and can be transferred to any time, city and cultural environment. Contemporary examples of the genre include *City of God* (Fernando Meirelles 2002) and *Kill Bill* (Quentin Tarantino 2003).
- Gangster films often have a drama documentary treatment, with the emphasis on realism.
- Landmark gangster movies include: *Underworld* (Joseph Von Sternberg 1927), *City Streets* (Rouben Mamoulian 1931), *Little Caesar* (Mervyn Le Roy 1931), *The Public Enemy* (William Wellman 1931), *Scarface* (Howard Hawks 1932, remade in 1983 by Brian De Palma), *Bonnie and Clyde* (Arthur Penn 1967), *The Godfather* trilogy (Francis Ford Coppola 1971–90), *Goodfellas* (Martin Scorsese 1990), *Reservoir Dogs* (Quentin Tarantino 1990), *Casino* (Martin Scorsese 1995) and *Gangs of New York* (Martin Scorsese 2003). This last film is 'retro-gangster', in that it traces the origins of gang violence in the early days of the city's foundation.
- Variants on gangster films include the British black comedy *Lock, Stock and Two Smoking Barrels* (Guy Ritchie 1998) and *Snatch* (Guy Ritchie 2000); a psychodrama variant is *Sexy Beast* (Jonathan Glazer 2001).

Narrative ingredients that make gangster films attractive to audiences

- The rise of ordinary individuals to positions of power, fame and success means that characters are easy to identify with and relate to, providing escapist fantasy for the audience.
- Action scenes with extreme violence grab audience attention.
- Love stories and family relationships are used as background.
- Use of the classic rise and fall narrative or 'nemesis' — retribution for evil-doing.
- Antihero status — bad guys are more interesting than good guys.
- The narrative can be transferred to any time, place and culture.
- Realism — storylines often run parallel to real life events.

Iconography of gangster films

- Fast cars
- Guns
- Smart suits
- Attractive and desirable women
- Glamorous lifestyle settings for the successful gangster

Narrative theory

Narrative theories look for common features present in all texts and explore their relationship to the attitudes, beliefs and values of the cultures from which they are drawn.

Propp, Vladimir (1895–1970)

Propp was a Russian formalist writer and folklorist, who analysed the structure of folk stories in *The Morphology of the Folktale*. He emphasised the role of character in structuring narrative and identified key characters that he claimed were present in all folk tales. These include:

- the **hero**, who seeks something
- the **villain**, who opposes the hero's quest
- the **donor**, who provides an object with magic properties
- the **dispatcher**, who sends the hero on his way
- the **false hero**, who disrupts the hero's hope of reward
- the **helper**, who aids the hero
- the **princess** — the reward for the hero and an object of the villain's schemes
- her **father**, who rewards the hero for his efforts

Although it is not advisable to try to locate all of Propp's characters in every story, a brief analysis of any James Bond movie will identify most of the above.

Todorov, Tzvetan (1939–)

Todorov is a Bulgarian intellectual of the Russian formalist school, living and writing in France since the mid-1960s. He emphasises the common basis of human experience and the underlying narrative behind all human activity. His sequence is based on five propositions, outlining a basic state of narration that is disturbed and then re-established:

- a state of equilibrium where everything is in order
- a disruption of the order by an event
- a recognition that a disruption has occurred
- an attempt to repair the damage of the disruption
- a return to equilibrium

It is easy to apply Todorov's theory to a wide range of narratives. Take the disaster movie *Earthquake* (Mark Robson 1974) as an example:

- equilibrium: life before the earthquake, with narratives involving relationships and community
- disruption: the earthquake
- recognition of the magnitude of the disaster
- emergency services and heroes go into action to rescue and repair
- aftermath: rescued characters and surviving heroes return to a kind of equilibrium

Lévi-Strauss, Claude (1908–)

Lévi-Strauss, a French structural anthropologist, analysed culture and myth and argued for a common origin of all narratives based on shared human life experience, fears and expectations.

Using techniques developed by Saussure he identified the structures of all myths as being the same and based on what he termed **binary opposition.** This he defined as the essential differences between such concepts as raw and cooked, good and evil, light and dark, insiders (of the tribe) and outsiders (the alien or other).

Narratives are based on oppositional forces and the resolution of conflict. Audiences are positioned on the side that justifies their own cultural values and resolution reduces underlying anxiety about threats to their way of life.

Lévi-Strauss's categories apply easily to most narratives and genres: cowboys and Indians, black hats and white hats, gangsters and police, and in newspaper and television news coverage — for example, demonstrators and the police or terrorists and coalition forces in Iraq. It is important to consider the positioning of the audience by asking the question 'whose side are we on and why?'

Barthes, Roland (1915–80)

Barthes was a French semiologist who identified five different codes by which a narrative engages the attention of an audience. In order of importance, these are:

- the enigma code — the audience is intrigued by the need to solve a problem
- the action code — the audience is excited by the urgent need to resolve a conflict
- the semantic code — the audience is directed towards an additional meaning by way of connotation
- the symbolic code — the audience assumes that a character dressed in black is evil or menacing and forms expectations of his/her behaviour on this basis
- the cultural code — the audience derives meaning in a text from shared cultural knowledge about the way the world works; this often takes the form of truisms found in proverbial sayings, for example evil doers are punished, a fool and his money are soon parted and what goes around comes around

These codes operate on the level of connotation and myth, which engage and sustain the audience's interest and attention.

Barthes's work is useful in explaining how audiences become intrigued and culturally engaged with narratives, through being drawn into problem solving, seeking resolution of conflict and seeing the values of their own lives and culture symbolically represented before them.

All crime narratives involve the enigma code.

1.4 Media audiences

Audience theory

Audience theories are attempts to explain the ways in which exposure to mass media texts affects or influences an audience's attitudes, beliefs, values and behaviour.

Stimulus-response theory: behaviourist psychology

This theory derives from the Russian physiologist Ivan Pavlov's famous conditioning of a dog who was trained to respond by salivating when a bell associated with the arrival of food was rung.

- In advertising, this can be seen in the simple association of an object of desire with a product, such as a girl in a bikini used to advertise a can of beer.
- The stimulus-response approach is the basis of the hypodermic theory (see p. 80).
- Although contemporary theories of audience responses to media content are more sophisticated, the power of suggestion by association is still widely used in advertising.

Active audience theories

An active audience theory is one that assumes audiences play an active part both in the selecting of media texts appropriate to their needs and in interpreting those texts in line with their own cultural perspectives. Active audiences are seen as empowered in their engagement with media texts rather than merely passive consumers.

Uses and gratifications theory

This theory, developed by Jay Blumler and Elihu Katz (1975), is in the active tradition and derives from a liberal, pluralist model of the media. It focuses on what people do with the media rather than what the media does to people. Audiences are seen as being free to pick and choose from a large number of available media products to satisfy their own needs.

Individuals may seek:
- diversion in the form of escape from reality
- emotional release of pleasure
- personal relationships through companionship and sociability
- knowledge of television characters, in order to interact with others
- personal identity and a sense of self worth through being members of a particular audience
- surveillance through finding out about the world and the events that affect them

Criticism of the theory

Although this is useful as an active theory that emphasises choices made by audiences and their control of their media consumption, it assumes that all audience needs are identified and met by the media and it underestimates the media's role in generating those needs in the first place.

Audience studies (also known as reception theory)

- This is an active audience theory associated with the work of John Fiske, Michel de Certeau and David Morley, which sees the audience as being actively engaged in the interpretation of media texts, rather than as passive consumers.
- Audiences decode media texts in ways that relate to their social and cultural circumstances and individual experiences.
- The theory uses qualitative and ethnographic methods, such as group interviews and participant observation, to assess audience responses.
- David Morley's research in 1980 of the audience for *Nationwide* (an evening current affairs programme) found that the audience's response to the subject matter of media texts was influenced by family, class and educational factors with the subject matter. For example, a group of management trainees saw the programme's items on trade unions as being biased towards the unions whereas a group of workers saw the same items as being anti-union. Different groups therefore interpreted texts in different ways according to their background and level of involvement.
- Morley developed the terms 'dominant', 'negotiated' and 'oppositional readings' to categorise responses.
- In the 1990s, the approach was developed by David Buckingham and termed 'new audience research'. Buckingham concentrated on children and concluded that by the age of seven they have become skilled readers of media texts and are able to interpret, challenge and reject media messages.

Criticism of the theory

- The approach is currently the most effective means of assessing the complex responses of sophisticated audiences in a media-saturated environment. However, the presence of a media researcher could be seen as partly determining the kinds of responses given by participants in the research.

- The research subjects, aware that they are under scrutiny, could modify their behaviour and responses in the same way that participants in questionnaires try to give what they think are the right or preferred answers to researchers.

Cultural effects theory

This is an active audience theory associated with the work of Stuart Hall and David Morley, which argues that there are gradual effects on an audience's attitudes, beliefs and values as the result of long-term exposure to media content, and that this tends to work in the interests of dominant ideology and the dominant reading of a text. However, audiences are able to challenge these preferred readings of media texts with their own negotiated or oppositional readings, which are based on their unique personal, social and cultural viewpoint.

Criticism of the theory

- Hall's approach is in the Marxist tradition, which sees the media as working in the interests of the ruling class to support dominant ideology and sustain the hegemonic position of the ruling elite. In this sense, the audience is passive, in that in the long term it is forced into the hegemonic common sense viewpoint of media texts.
- In traditional Marxist analysis, such as the highly pessimistic Frankfurt School, the masses are seen as helpless victims of media manipulation, lost in false consciousness and with no real power to subvert media messages or challenge ruling elites.
- With the breakdown of traditional political, paternalistic and authoritarian structures in western societies, and with the development of sophisticated consumer lifestyle marketing and advertising applied to all aspects of life and personal identity, it can be argued that the majority population is more manipulated than ever before.
- In allowing for the subversive undermining of preferred readings of texts and their substitution by negotiated or oppositional readings, Hall assumes an active response from those marginalised by the ruling elite, such as ethnic minorities, who are thus able to form a counterculture of resistance.
- In 2005, suburban riots among the disadvantaged ethnic minority youths of many French cities were accompanied by a total rejection of French values, language and culture as expressed through the French media. Over recent years, this has been accompanied by the adoption of an oppositional value system and slang language (*sabir*). Violently alternative anti-police and anti-state rap music, popular with the rioters, has also been under investigation in France for its role in encouraging the counterculture violence.
- In increasingly ethnically diverse and fragmented postmodern societies, Hall's approach identifies closely with the increasing challenge to dominant western ideology presented by sub-cultures, ethnic groups and even fundamentalists following an altogether different ideology.

Passive effects theories

The effects tradition is largely passive and emphasises what the media does to the audience. The approach tends to underestimate the ability of audiences to challenge and negotiate the meanings of media texts from their own unique viewpoint.

Hypodermic theory

This early media theory, originating in the 1930s in the Frankfurt School of political philosophy in Germany, assumes a direct stimulus–response relationship between audience reactions and the consumption of media texts. The media texts act like a drug

being injected into the passive audience and audience behaviour is seen as being directly affected.

The theory is often used when debating sex and violence in the media to argue for a direct link between the viewing of media texts and behaviour. It was particularly useful in the 1930s and 1940s in helping to explain the operation of the propaganda machines of Stalinist Russia and Nazi Germany.

Criticism of the theory

- It was modelled on the submission of the German population to the propaganda of the Nazis and their apparently uncritical acceptance of the excesses of the regime and their disastrous consequences. This model of the audience does not allow for any meaningful resistance to media messages and pays insufficient attention to the physically coercive methods used to enforce acceptance of the regime.
- In exile in the USA, Frankfurt School members were European elitists who deplored the industrialisation of culture by what they called the 'culture industry' and the emerging forms of popular culture, which they saw as a shallow and vulgar manipulation of mass sentiment for profit. They underestimated the dynamic nature of US society.
- The theory is now seen as far too simplistic to explain the complex relationships that exist between contemporary media texts and widely diverse audiences.

Inoculation theory

This was advanced by investigators of the impact of sensational images involving sex and violence, and suggests that the more audiences are exposed to violent or sexual imagery, the more indifferent to it they become and the more likely they are to see violent and sexual acts as normal behaviour. The audience is — in effect — inoculated against it and is no longer shocked by violent or sexual scenes.

This indifference in turn encourages media producers to push the limits further and further in order to create sensation, and theorists argue that this ultimately leads to a breakdown of all restraint.

The theory features in discussions of so-called copycat violence, where individuals are accused of acting out violent scenes from films in real life. For example, the child murderers of toddler Jamie Bulger in 1993 were said to have watched the film *Child's Play 3*, which gave them the idea of the murder, although no real evidence was produced in court that the boys had seen the film.

The 2003 French film *Irreversible* (Gaspar Noé 2003) contains a 10 minute actual time rape scene, followed by hideous violence committed against the woman who had been raped. It has been accused of pure sensationalism and of pushing the boundaries of acceptable film making to the limits, bordering on sexually violent pornography.

Criticism of the theory

- This is the approach adopted by those seeking media censorship — for example, pressure groups like Mediawatch-UK (formerly the National Viewers' and Listeners' Association, founded in 1965 by Mary Whitehouse, a campaigner against sex and violence on television). Such organisations seek the reintroduction of censorship to return to some golden age of 'family values'.
- Investigators like Aston University's Guy Cumberbatch have consistently argued that those who claim **empirical** evidence for a cause-and-effect relationship between

media representations of sex and violence and behaviour have no worthwhile evidence to support their views.

empiricism: a research method based on the measuring and testing of observable evidence, and when applied to media effects it often claims scientific status. However, it is important to pay careful attention to the research methods used as these can often be based on biased, limited or ambiguous criteria that are then used by researchers to draw exaggerated, far-reaching and unjustifiable conclusions for their results.

Cultivation theory

Audience research in the effects tradition was initiated by the American George Gerbner in the 1960s. Gerbner conducted research on how watching television affects people's views of the real world, and concluded that television has long-term effects that are small and gradual but cumulative and, ultimately, significant.

Television tends to reinforce values already present in a culture and supports dominant ideology.

Cultivation theory is particularly interested in the representation of sex and violence and whether or not this influences audience behaviour.

Criticism of the theory

Being in the passive audience tradition, unlike more recent developments in the effects approach, the theory does not allow for an oppositional reading by the viewer or for the audience's social position, and existing attitudes, beliefs and values, which may influence the ways the individuals interpret media content.

Two-step flow theory

This passive theory devised by Elihu Katz and Paul Lazarsfeld in 1955 represented a move away from the classic stimulus–response principles that had dominated audience theories during the 1940s.

The first stage involves people called 'opinion leaders', with influential status in society. The message is then passed by these leaders to the second stage — a larger audience. The mass audience's willingness or receptiveness to the message is seen as being influenced by the status of the opinion leaders.

Opinion leaders were traditionally seen as those with high status in society, such as politicians, clergymen and academics, but in contemporary society they are more likely to be footballers, pop stars or reality television celebrities.

Criticism of the theory
- The theory postulates a hierarchy of consumption of media texts that in reality does not exist.
- Individuals access a wide range of media products, from mobile phone texts to the internet, television channels and print media, and do not depend on others to act as mediators.
- More important than opinion leaders are the mediated representations of the media itself, which can only offer a partial and often distorted view of the world.
- In spite of massive efforts by the British government propaganda machine in trying to lead public opinion in the justification of the Iraq invasion in 2003, through

claiming expertise, specialised knowledge and secret alarming reports of weapons of mass destruction, the venture remained deeply unpopular with a sceptical British public, which suggests that 'opinion leaders' have less power than previously thought.

What do audiences derive from media texts?

Media texts meet the needs of an audience by:

- providing information
- contributing towards personal growth and development
- providing entertainment and escapism
- creating a sense of social and cultural involvement and belonging
- giving pleasure
- giving a sense of control and empowerment

Maslow's hierarchy of human need (1954)

Psychologist Abraham Maslow's hierarchy of human need suggests that the fulfilment of needs works like a pyramid, where satisfaction at the most basic or lowest level is necessary before the next stage can be reached. Consumption of media texts fulfils needs at all levels above the lowest two — the satisfaction of basic survival and safety needs — and can help explain what satisfaction or pleasure audiences derive from different media texts (see Figure 2).

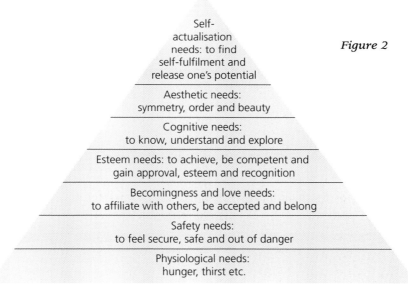

Figure 2

The system does not allow for the escapist function of media texts — where audiences seek to forget their current condition and escape to a world of fantasy and make-believe where their lives are often transformed or improved.

Even those at the lowest level of Maslow's pyramid may seek psychological wellbeing as relief or distraction from physical discomfort and fear in this way.

Vance Packard's eight needs

American cultural analyst Vance Packard (*The Hidden Persuaders* 1957) developed Maslow's theory to explore the way in which advertisers exploit and manipulate human needs to sell their products. He identified eight 'needs':

- emotional security
- ego gratification

- reassurance of personal worth or value
- to give and receive love and affection
- to be creative
- for power and control
- to identify roots and origins
- to feel immortal

These criteria can be used to help explain what audiences derive from the consumption of media texts.

EXAMINER'S TIP

When discussing theories of audience behaviour and the media, remember that all theories are speculative and usually draw conclusions based on selective research. They are not proven by this research to be either true or false, so try to avoid claiming in examination essays that an example or piece of research 'proves' a theory. It does not.

2 | Specification focus: OCR Unit 2732 (AS)

This is the case study part of the OCR specification. There is a choice of two topics offered by OCR. Centres must choose one topic to prepare you in advance for the case study examination. In the exam, there are *four* questions on each topic from which you must answer a total of *three*.

The topics are set by the examination board and can change each year. They are currently:
- New media technologies
- Media ownership

Preparation for this unit will depend on the topic offered by OCR and the choice made by centres, so these notes cannot be more specific. You should approach your teacher or lecturer for more details on this unit. However, all the notes and advice on the use of key concepts apply to the case study material.

CHAPTER 5 *Media issues and debates*

This chapter focuses on OCR Unit 2735 (A2) but the material covered is of value to those studying other specifications.

1 Specification focus: OCR Unit 2735 (A2)

The OCR specification requires you to answer *one* question from each of the three main media forms: **broadcasting**, **film** and **print**, drawing on your knowledge and understanding of all the key concepts. Nine questions are offered, with one to be answered from each section — a total of three questions in all. The topics covered are subject to alteration.

1.1 Broadcasting

The OCR topics for the 2006 examination series were:
- British television soap operas
- Radio and television news
- British broadcasting since 1990

For the 2007 examinations, the topics are:
- Music programmes on television
- Broadcast news and current affairs
- Contemporary British broadcasting

Issues in broadcasting

Ownership and control

Media ownership is an important issue because of the power of the media to set agendas, direct public attention, shape opinion and ultimately to influence behaviour. Those in power can use the media to maintain their position and achieve hegemony.
- Former Italian Prime Minister Silvio Berlusconi had a controlling interest in Italian television and media companies and his opponents claimed that he had used this power to advance his own party political interests.
- During the debate over the Iraq war, all the newspapers and television channels controlled by the News Corporation and Rupert Murdoch presented similar uncritical support for the US and British action.

In Britain, media ownership is subject to government scrutiny to limit monopoly power.

The digital revolution

The advent of the set-top digital box and the reality of multi-channel television are transforming the viewer's relationship with the traditional television channels. Televisions and computers are becoming interchangeable, with digital channels accessible online.

Minority/narrowcast

The large number of channels available via digital television allows for narrowcasting, with channels focused on particular niche audiences and interests. Examples include religious broadcasting, music, sports, history and adult sex channels. Although some of these channels are available on Freeview, many are available as a paid-for top-up television option or subscription.

Accountability and censorship watchdog bodies: the role of Ofcom

Ofcom is the public body responsible for regulating television, radio and telecommunications media in the UK. It replaced the Independent Television Commission, the

Broadcasting Standards Council, the Radio Authority and the Radio Communications Agency under the terms of the 2003 communications act. Its remit does not currently include the BBC.

Complaints to Ofcom about media content tend to be about offence caused by language, sex and violence and the regulator is particularly concerned to monitor the 9 p.m. watershed; other frequent complaints regard religious offence, homophobic or racist content, inaccuracy and impartiality.

The regulator publishes regular bulletins with details of complaints, the response of the broadcasters and conclusions.

Sponsorship and advertising

- Commercial broadcasting channels are facing growing dilemmas with the future of advertising as their prime source of revenue. Conventional television advertising is in decline as new technology, such as Sky+ and TiVo, allows viewers to bypass advertising breaks between programmes.
- Fragmented audiences mean that fewer people are likely to be watching conventional adverts.
- Shrinkage in television advertising will mean falling revenues for commercial broadcasters. In 2005, television advertising revenue fell by 3.5%, whereas internet advertising increased by 73%.
- The broadcasters would like to make **product placement** deals with advertisers — a practice that would blur the line between advertising and broadcasting. This proposal is not popular with the regulator Ofcom.
- Branding is already a part of our daily lives and is regularly reflected on the screen by sponsorship deals, particularly of sporting events, linking the event with a commercial company. One example is Six Nations Rugby, which is sponsored by the Royal Bank of Scotland.
- Advertisers are looking for ways of using branded celebrities and new bands to identify products on ads carried by mobile phones; they are developing **Mobisoaps** — soap opera style advertising narratives available on mobile phones — as a new way of reaching an audience.
- New forms of product placement may help make commercial broadcasters become more commercially viable in a highly competitive market. There could be an increase in the number of sponsors listed at the end of entertainment programmes to include those whose products have featured in the programme.

TERMINOLOGY

Product placement: the positioning of a product as part of the setting/props for a drama or entertainment programme, such as Perrier mineral water or Red Bull clearly identifiable on the table in a restaurant scene.

The future of Public Service Broadcasting

Public Service Broadcasting (PSB) is based on the idea that the broadcast media play such a vital role in providing a society with information, education and entertainment that they take on cultural importance. This role requires that broadcasting should be seen as a public service, subsidised and regulated by the state rather than by a commercially based profit-making enterprise.

PSB is often associated with the views of Lord Reith, the first Director General of the BBC, who saw the corporation's role as being to 'inform, instruct and entertain' the public. In the UK, this ethos has influenced government policy towards the media, but the future of this philosophy is being questioned in the age of digital, multi-channel television.

The BBC benefits from having both an extensive commercial dimension and the guaranteed support of the licence fee — a competitive position that operators like Sky regard as unfair. At the time of writing, the government intends to maintain the licence fee for the BBC, but requires a quality monitoring of its output to ensure that its activities and investments are in the best interest of its viewers. The government also plans to replace the current board of governors with a new body to ensure public accountability.

Public access

With the broadcasting media being controlled by a large hierarchical and commercial organisation, it is important that ordinary people should be able to get their point of view across without having it filtered by institutions. Increasingly, this is made possible by technological developments that allow individuals to express their opinions via the internet, interactive digital television and through the provision of public access slots for opinions and video diaries.

Programme quality/dumbing down

- The large increase in available channels does not necessarily mean better quality or even greater choice.
- Financial pressures and intense competition squeeze programme budgets and encourage television operators to fill the schedules with old films, cheap reality television and repeats.
- Competition for limited advertising revenues means that company finances are under pressure and this is often blamed for poor quality of programming, as production budgets are cut.
- Live *Big Brother* transmissions can consist of a camera fixed for 20 minutes on a sleeping contestant and some programmes consist of broadcasting police surveillance tapes.

Regulation/deregulation

This was an issue in the 1990s, when deregulation legislation (Broadcasting Act 1990) was introduced by the Conservative government. Many commentators and journalists argued that the market economy applied to the broadcast media would lead to increased concentration of media ownership in the hands of a few powerful companies and a decline in programme quality as a result of market pressure to reduce costs and increase profits.

The issue of protection of the BBC from the rigours of the free market by the granting of its license fee remains, with competitors such as Sky claiming that the current situation represents unfair competition and arguing for the total commercial independence of the BBC.

Sample topic: British television soap operas

Principal British soaps

EastEnders

Hollyoaks

Emmerdale

Coronation Street

Characteristics of soap operas

Soap operas are continuing serials characterised by:

- a fixed location in the present
- everyday settings: streets, bars, pubs, restaurants, schools, shops, homes
- a range of characters
- multiple parallel narratives
- cliffhanger endings
- regular scheduling

Questions and answers

Q: Why do institutions produce soap operas?

A: the magnetic and addictive appeal of soap operas to their fans guarantees a successful soap a mass audience and high viewer ratings

Q: Why do people watch soap operas?

A:
- They run parallel to people's lives and reflect the concerns and problems of everyday life.
- They provide a topic of discussion and constantly feature in the tabloid press.
- They can become addictive and an obsession once the audiences are engaged with plot lines and with the cliffhangers, leaving them desperate to find out how dilemmas are resolved.
- They offer surrogate friendships and relationships: audiences feel that they know characters personally and take a close interest in their development.
- They discuss moral dilemmas and issues facing people in everyday life.
- Narratives often have an **enigma** structure — for example, in *Hollyoaks*: will Mel stop drinking? Will Tony tell Becca's husband Jake of her affair with Justin? (Examples from soap operas like these date very quickly, so think of some contemporary narratives that involve enigmas.)
- They cover a multiplicity of intense experiences concentrated into a limited time frame.
- Although they mirror everyday life, the lives of soap characters involve more excitement, action and conflict than are usually present in ordinary lives.
- They allow audiences to take sides on issues of behaviour and moral judgement.
- They are voyeuristic — audiences take pleasure in looking in on domestic relationships and problems.
- Actors become national celebrities and role models, whose real personalities are often confused with their screen characters.
- Storylines are resolved, but the soaps go on and are always changing, with characters entering and leaving.
- They provide escapism and a regular point of routine and reference in people's lives.

Soap operas and gender

Soap operas are watched by more women than men. Researchers Dorothy Hobson (*Crossroads: The Drama of a Soap Opera*, 1982) and Ann Gray (*Studying Culture: An Introductory Reader*, Gray and McEuigan 1993) have suggested that women probably prefer open-ended narratives, whereas men prefer the closed narrative of crime fiction.

Christine Geraghty (*Women and Soap Operas: A Study of Prime Time Soaps*, 1991) classified soaps as 'women's fiction' because:

- they are concerned with personal relationships
- they have strong female leads

- they are centred on domestic life
- they provide escapism

Soap operas and social issues

Soaps, particularly those directed at an audience of young people, can be used in a public service or public information role to air concerns viewers may have over sensitive issues of welfare or behaviour.

Phil Redmond is responsible for the long running school soap opera, *Grange Hill* and for the Channel 4 soaps *Brookside* and *Hollyoaks*. When *Brookside* was launched as the new soap for Channel 4 in November 1982, Redmond was concerned that the soap, set in Liverpool, should have a formula that blended 'entertainment with the raising of social issues'. ITV's *Coronation Street*, which had done so much to legitimise the representation of working class lives on television in the 1960s, had become an institution but seemed increasingly out of touch with social realities. *Brookside*, set on a new, purpose-built estate, tackled controversial issues and reflected current social values and concerns. In the intense competition between soap operas for viewers, it lost direction in its search to sensationalise storylines, and with falling ratings (it fell from a peak of 7 million viewers to just 1.5 million) it was banished from prime time viewing to Saturday afternoon and was finally axed by Channel 4 in November 2003 after 21 years.

With the ending of *Brookside,* the teen soap *Hollyoaks*, set in Chester, was boosted to run every weekday evening at 6.30 p.m., with the next episode available as a preview on 4 digital. It features the same formula of entertainment and social issues.

Brookside ran storylines involving rape, incest, lesbianism, racism, drug addiction, drug-related crime and mental illness.

Hollyoaks has run storylines covering:
- self-harm
- date-rape drugs
- Obsessive Compulsive Disorder (OCD)
- alcoholism
- wrongful arrest and imprisonment
- credit card fraud
- student debt
- student/teacher relationships
- sexual experimentation and peer group pressure
- epilepsy
- meningitis awareness
- abortion
- cot death

Reasons for the success of Hollyoaks
- It has a cast of glamorous young people — including *Hollyoaks* 'babes', who attract a male audience, with spin-off coverage in lads' mags, and produce workout videos for girls.
- The transience of university life, which forms the background of many characters, allows for a steady introduction and removal of characters before they go stale.
- It has a good mixture of age ranges in its characters.
- It has developed high production values, with film treatment software giving a glossy and polished feel to the production.

- It has a high standard of camera work and editing.
- It balances light-hearted, comic plot elements with serious and controversial issues.
- The treatment fits perfectly with teen lifestyle magazines and mainstream youth culture.
- Plot lines are relevant, sometimes edgy and usually well developed..
- Acting standards are generally high..
- The early evening prime-time slot catches the audience before it goes out.

1.2 Film

The OCR examination topics for 2006 were:
- British cinema since 1990
- The concept of genre in film
- Censorship and film

For examinations in 2007, the topics are:
- Contemporary British cinema
- The concept of genre in film
- Censorship and film

Issues in film

Dominance of big corporate companies

Big budget blockbusters dominate the film scene, with corporate companies controlling production and distribution. Critics argue that this works in favour of formulaic and uninspired productions and remakes, and against the development of new, creative talent operating under low budget constraints.

The big ten Hollywood film studios are Twentieth Century Fox (News Corporation), MGM (Sony), DreamWorks, Miramax (Disney), Sony Pictures (Sony), Paramount, Universal (Vivendi), New Line Cinema (Time Warner), Walt Disney Pictures (Disney) and Warner Brothers (Time Warner). Six giant corporations control the bulk of film production and distribution.

Independent alternative cinema

The outlets provided by DVD and internet release are seen by some as a benefit to small producers, who can use blogs to publicise their products. *The Blair Witch Project* (Daniel Myrick 1999) was an early example of a low budget production that relied on internet publicity to build an audience.

American world dominance

US media corporations dominate the world market, leading to claims of cultural imperialism. In spite of the power of the big multinational corporations, national cinema has traditionally been strong. It continues to develop in India, China, Japan and South America and is growing in importance in Africa.

Survival of national cinema in the UK (Britfilm)

- National cinema industries in Europe survive to varying degrees with tax breaks and government support.
- The UK Film Council is charged with lobbying government and media organisations on behalf of the British film industry.
- Film makers have to be increasingly resourceful and ingenious to put together packages to finance their projects from the various sources of available funds.

- The BBC has funded such hits as *Billy Elliot* (Stephen Daldry 2000) and is planning to double the funding for BBC Films over 2 years, providing a welcome additional source of finance.
- Channel 4's Film4 company was founded to support film development and is responsible for film hits such as *Four Weddings and a Funeral* (Mike Newell 1994) and *East is East* (Damien O'Donnell 1999).

Emergence of cinema in the developing world

Cinema from developing countries is an important source of new cultural perspectives and creativity. It often takes the voice of the dispossessed and serves to highlight social and political inequalities and injustices — for example, *City of God* (Fernando Meirelles 2002), set in South America.

Representation of violence and sex

The mainstream representation of sex in the context of positive relationships, for example in *Nine Songs* (Michael Winterbottom 2005), although still controversial, is no longer an issue for the censor, but some concern remains over the representation of violent sex.

The portrayal of a violent rape in real time in the French film *Irreversible* (Gaspar Noé 2003) did not prevent its release with an 18 rating in some UK cinemas. The representation of horrific fantasy violence not involving sex, while attracting comment from organisations like Mediawatch-UK, seems not to be of general public concern.

Decline in multiplex audiences

The long period of success for the multiplex cinema complexes may be under threat as audiences show signs of decline in the face of competition from home cinema, DVD and internet outlets.

The industry's response has been to announce an increase in allocation for low budget films with art house and minority appeal. *Brokeback Mountain* (Ang Lee 2005) produced high returns on a low budget, using a gay storyline in a western setting.

Sample topic: censorship and film

Censorship is the practice, exercised by elite groups in authority, of monitoring and controlling media content by removing, suppressing or classifying elements deemed offensive or subversive for moral, political, economic, social or religious reasons.

Historical context of censorship debates

- The British Board of Film Censors was established in 1912 to standardise the censorship and classification of films in the UK.
- The first issues in film censorship related to the horror genre and the classification H for horror to restrict showing to over 16s.
- The X certificate replaced the H in the UK in 1951.
- Relaxation of censorship in the 1960s and the abolition of the Hays Committee in the USA led to an increase in the graphic representation of sex and violence in film.
- The X certificate rating was raised to 18 in 1971.
- Pro-censorship groups like the National Viewers' and Listeners' Association (now Mediawatch-UK) and religious activists in the Festival of Light challenged specific films, notably *Trash* (Andy Warhol 1970), *Last Tango in Paris* (Bernardo Bertolucci 1972), *The Exorcist* (William Friedkin 1973) and *The Devils* (Ken Russell 1971).

- The X certificate was replaced by the 18 classification in 1982. The VHS recorder made violent and pornographic video productions much easier to reproduce and distribute.
- In 1984, the Video Recordings Act was passed in response to the appearance of so-called 'video nasties' (a list kept by the Director of Public Prosecutions — for example, *Driller Killer* (Abel Ferrara 1979)). It required all videos for hire to be subject to censorship and a classification system.
- During the 1980s, the British authorities attempted to suppress pornographic material legally available in many European countries, driving video pornography underground.
- The British Board of Film Classification (BBFC) replaced the British Board of Film Censors in 1985 with a wider brief covering video recordings.
- In 1994, in response to public and press reaction to the killing of toddler Jamie Bulger by children who may have seen a video of the film *Child's Play 3* (Jack Bender 1991), the Criminal Justice and Public Order Act was passed, tightening the BBFC's assessment criteria to include the word 'harm' in relation to the portrayal of sexual, violent, horrific, criminal or drug-related behaviour.
- During the 1990s, the attitude of the authorities to pornography was relaxed, with the R18 rating used to classify pornographic material for sale to adults via licensed outlets.
- Easy access to extreme forms of pornography via the internet is a concern, particularly in relation to children and minors. Child protection legislation makes it illegal to own or access child pornography. There is debate over government plans to introduce legislation to criminalise the accessing and possession of images of extreme sexual violence and bestiality.

The Hays code

This production code was established in 1930 by the Hays Office. The Hays Office was a self-regulating body, set up by the US film industry in 1922 under the chairmanship of William H. Hays, which listed forbidden subjects and scenes. The code was abolished in 1967.

Current film classification

The BBFC is the organisation responsible for classifying and certifying films, DVDs and videos for public showing and — in the case of videos and DVDs — also for private viewing.

It sees its role as providing classification within acceptable guidelines rather than censorship. It has been involved in liberalising restrictions on visual material directed at adult audiences. Films are classified by the BBFC under the following categories:

Uc suitable for pre-school children
U suitable for those aged 4 and over
PG suitable for children of any age, but parental guidance should be given
12a no child under 12 may see the film unless accompanied by an adult
12 suitable viewing for those aged 12 and over
15 suitable viewing for those aged 15 and over
18 suitable viewing for those aged 18 and over
R18 category reserved for sexually explicit material available to adults in licensed sex shops

Criteria for classification

- Classification is based on the number and type of swear words, and the amount of sex and violence, sexual violence or drug taking that the film contains.
- The principal concern is the protection of children and young people from material deemed harmful or corrupting.
- Certain four letter words would be allowed once in a film rated 12; any more instances would result in a 15 certificate.
- The classifications can create controversy: Ken Loach's film *Sweet Sixteen* (2002) was refused a 15 certificate even though it was acted by, and targeted at, 15–16 year olds, because it contained a four letter word that is still regarded by the board as unacceptable for an under-18 audience.
- Classification of videos and DVDs for home viewing can be more severe than for cinema because of the private nature of the viewing environment. It is argued that the public nature of cinema exhibition has a modifying effect on reactions to violent and sexually explicit material, which is not present when the material is viewed privately.
- Films can be controversial, usually in relation to the representation of sex and violence. Examples include the French film *Baise-moi* (Virginie Despentes and Coralie 2000), which includes a sexually explicit rape scene and an orgy of sexually violent revenge; the French film *Irreversible* (Gaspar Noé 2003), which records a horrific scene of sexual violence and rape in real time; and *Nine Songs* (Michael Winterbottom 2005), which graphically and explicitly narrates a loving, sexual relationship against a background of pop music concerts.

Issues in censorship

- The movement in western societies towards liberalisation of sexual material for over 18s, while protecting children, has blurred the distinction between hard core pornographic material and mainstream entertainment.
- The internet has massively increased the audience for pornography. Are children adequately protected? Should there be increased censorship and control of the internet, particularly in relation to images involving sadistic violence and bestiality? Should new criminal offences in relation to the downloading of internet pornography be created?
- Does exposure to explicit images of sex and violence encourage copycat behaviour?
- Are audiences desensitised by exposure to violent and sexual images?
- Should images be censored for religious reasons or for causing offence to minority groups?
- How should liberal western societies manage relationships with minority groups and religions who demand total censorship of all images of the unclothed human body?

1.3 Print

The OCR topics for this section in 2006 were:

- Magazines and gender
- Local newspapers
- Freedom, regulation and control of the British press

For examinations in 2007, the topics are:

- The magazine industry
- Local newspapers
- Freedom, regulation and control

Print media include newspaper publishers (considered on pp. 54–60) and magazine publishers.

Magazine publishers in the UK

The magazine market is highly competitive and dynamic with over 3000 established titles. More than 1000 magazine launches are proposed each year. Of these, approximately 350 make it to publication and only half of these become established titles.

IPC Media

- Britain's largest magazine publisher, with over 100 titles and 22% of the market; it sells 350 million magazines a year
- Taken over by Time Warner in 2001
- Titles include *Loaded, Nuts, Marie Claire* and *NME*

Emap

- Second largest UK magazine publisher with 200 magazines and 16% of the market share
- Titles include *Bliss, More!, Heat, Zoo* and *FHM*

National Magazine Company (Natmag)

- Probably the largest magazine company in the world, with over a quarter of a billion copies sold per year
- 80 international editions sold in 100 countries
- Part of The Hearst Corporation in the USA
- British titles include *Cosmopolitan, Esquire, Good Housekeeping, She* and *Country Living*

Condé Nast

- Glossy magazine publisher that is part of a larger US operation
- Titles include *GQ, Vogue, Glamour, Tatler, Easy Living, House & Garden, Brides, The World of Interiors* and *Vanity Fair*

Dennis Publishing

- Independent, privately-owned publisher of *Maxim* (in 21 countries), *Men's Fitness, The Week, PC Pro, Custom PC, Viz, Test Drive* and *Bizarre*

Covers of lifestyle magazines

The cover of a typical lifestyle magazine usually has the following elements:

- issue number
- cover price
- bar code
- main cover line
- straplines
- feature article photographs
- puffs — self-boosting claims for the magazine

TERMINOLOGY

Strapline: this is a memorable phrase used in conjunction with a masthead brand or company name to emphasise what a company or product seeks to be identified with or remembered by. Examples include 'The future's bright, the future's Orange' for Orange phone ads and '*Vorsprung durch Technik*' (progress through technology) for Audi cars.

Content

Lifestyle magazines will contain combinations of the following:

- advertising
- advertising features
- agony columns/advice
- campaigns
- competitions/quizzes
- confessions
- contents pages
- contents of next issue
- diaries
- editorial
- feature articles
- horoscopes
- letters
- makeovers
- merchandising
- opinion/attitude surveys
- opinion columns
- reviews
- supplements and give-aways
- true stories

Issues in print media

Corporate ownership

The concentration of media ownership in the hands of a few powerful conglomerate companies seems to have been accepted, regardless of concerns that independence of editorial judgement cannot always be guaranteed.

In spite of the wide range of opinions and the level of controversy aroused by the British and US decision to invade Iraq in 2003, all of the newspapers owned by the News Corporation (Rupert Murdoch) on three continents had broadly similar editorials supporting the war.

However, in spite of this concentration of ownership, there was a wide range of different opinion expressed in the British press during the Iraq war, suggesting the survival of pluralism.

'Tabloidisation' and declining circulations

With newspapers facing gently declining circulations and increasing competition from alternative media — particularly the internet and 24-hour news channels — there is a growing tendency towards entertainment and feature journalism with a broader appeal. This has led to claims of 'tabloidisation' and the dumbing down of serious content by quality newspapers as they adapt to a changing media environment.

Chequebook journalism

This involves paying individuals for the stories. Although newspapers deny 'chequebook journalism' in principle, in practice they continue to buy serial rights to famous and infamous memoirs in order to attract readers.

The invasion of privacy versus public interest

Newspapers often claim that their intrusion into people's private lives is in the public interest, especially where the behaviour and morals of celebrities and public figures is concerned. Individuals have little recourse other than to the Press Complaints Commission or the libel laws if they feel that their privacy has been violated or that they have been misrepresented. Libel actions are expensive and usually undertaken by only the very rich.

Individuals who have complaints upheld by the Press Complaints Commission are often disappointed by the limited coverage given by newspapers to an apology, compared with the size of the original story.

The cult of celebrity in magazine and newspaper journalism

Celebrity culture dominates the tabloid press and increasingly influences the contents of quality newspapers, at the expense of more serious journalism. Critics argue that this is part of the dumbing down process, where hard news is being replaced by soft news and 'infotainment'.

Lifestyle magazines for audiences and advertisers

Lifestyle magazines provide a lifestyle setting to attract audiences and advertisers. Audiences increasingly define their identity in terms of personal appearance, patterns of consumption, personal behaviour and relationships, and their chosen magazines reflect their self-image and aspirations.

The magazines' mixture of advertising copy with idealised lifestyle contexts provides audiences with escapism and advertisers with a sound platform for the products that promise to help achieve the reader's aspirations.

Regulation: the Press Complaints Commission (PCC)

This is the newspaper and magazine complaints body or 'watchdog' established in 1991 to monitor newspaper content in response to complaints by members of the public. Its structure was revised in 1993 following complaints concerning invasion of privacy.

The Commission is intended to provide recourse for those who feel that newspaper/magazine content has either offended or misrepresented them personally, or for those who have a view about the fairness or ethical nature of the content. It operates under a 16 point code of practice and if, after investigating a complaint, the Commission finds a newspaper or magazine at fault, it can require the newspaper to publish details of the judgement. The code of practice is under continual revision by a committee of newspaper editors.

The Commission often cites 'freedom of expression' and 'the public interest' as a justification for publishing controversial stories. It was instrumental in securing the agreement by newspapers to limit the intrusion into the lives of Princes William and Harry.

Sample topic: magazines and gender

Women's magazines

Lifestyle magazines have been directed at women since the early twentieth century, with their contents targeting what were seen as the housewife's concerns — care of her husband and family, personal appearance, cooking and domestic chores, knitting, sewing and general household maintenance.

This formula lasted until the 1960s, when changes in the status of women, the advent of the contraceptive pill and equal employment rights combined with the growing influence of the women's movement to bring about changes in the way women saw themselves and their lives.

Classic British women's magazines of the 1950s, some still being published, include *Woman and Home, Woman, Woman's Own* and *Woman's Weekly*. Magazines like *Vogue* were essentially fashion magazines directed at the wealthy.

Cosmopolitan (Cosmo)

Cosmopolitan was founded in 1972 and was the first of a new generation of women's magazine to recognise the dramatic changes that had taken place in women's lives

during the 1960s. Under the original editor, Helen Gurley Brown, it broke new ground in advocating sexual and economic freedom for women and in recognising that its readers were interested not only in men but also in appearance, mind, body and career.

The magazine was taken seriously by academics and supporters of the women's movement as an important contribution to the advancement of women's self confidence and independence. It became a symbol of the changing times by discussing all aspects of sexuality openly for the first time and was the first mainstream women's magazine to publish naked male pin-ups.

In spite of its high profile on social and women's issues, *Cosmopolitan* is essentially a consumer lifestyle magazine. Its high-spending readership make it a magnet for advertisers — its readers spend £1 billion a year on fashion goods and £1.4 billion on new cars.

Cosmopolitan is published in 28 countries and is owned by National Magazines, which also publishes *Esquire, Good Housekeeping, Harper's Bazaar, Cosmo Girl* and the US edition of *Marie Claire* under licence from the French title owner Hachette.

Girls' magazines

Girls' magazines have developed from the classic *Girl* newspaper in the 1950s to reflect changing social attitudes towards girlhood and sexuality.

Jackie

Jackie was launched in 1964 at the height of Beatlemania and, in the 1970s, dominated the market with its combination of agony column advice, reader's letters, photo-strip romance stories and pop star pin-ups

It reflected the greater innocence of the 1970s teenybopper culture, which concentrated on romance, fashion and beauty and saw itself as a big sister to its readers. Pin-ups were wholesome, not raunchy, and Donnie Osmond and David Cassidy were favourites.

Angela McRobbie's study of the magazine (*Jackie: An Ideology of Adolescent Femininity*, 1978, reprinted in 1991 as *Jackie Magazine: Romantic Individualism and the Teenage Girl*) found that it offered girls narrow horizons, reinforcing stereotypes in relationships, where girls were subservient and passive in relation to boys, and were only interested in engagement rings.

Careers advice was limited to traditional areas like beauty therapy, nursing or working with animals. Life revolved around getting a boyfriend, and letters to agony aunts Cathy and Clare were on subjects such as how to kiss and the problem of wearing glasses. Sex and sexuality, contraception and abortion were not covered. *Jackie* failed to adapt to changing social attitudes and closed in 1993.

Just Seventeen (J17)

Just Seventeen was launched by Nick Logan in 1983 and was published by Emap. It reflected the changes in social attitudes towards women and girls and was targeted at girls age 12–16 who aspired to the age of 17, with its connotations of maturity and excitement.

The magazine's contents identified with a readership interested in sex, future careers, celebrities, mobile phones, fashion and appearance. It also provided advice on sexual behaviour and relationships and in its day broke new ground with its frank and open discussion of sex and sexuality.

It closed in 2004 following declining sales and increased competition from a new generation of girls magazines, such as *Bliss* and *Sugar*. These magazines, launched in the twenty-first century, reflect the more sophisticated world of pre-teen and teen girls in the post-girlpower world. They deal frankly and explicitly with all aspects of sexuality and sexual behaviour.

Bliss

Bliss is published in A5 handbag size and is called a 'baby glossy'. It focuses on boys, music, beauty, fashion and teen issues and it claims to be Britain's first interactive magazine, with internet and mobile phone links throughout. **blissmag.co.uk** claims to be the number 1 magazine website, and offers *Bliss* by e-mail, text or on-line.

Bliss, read by girls aged 13–18, is worldly and sophisticated in its attitude to sex and relationships and all issues affecting self-presentation and identity. It connects with celebrity culture but also features articles on crime and world issues like climate change.

Bliss: content analysis

Issue: May 2006
Cover price: £2.20
Total number of pages: 162
Adverts: approximately 65 pages, with many advertisements tied in to beauty, appearance and fashion features.

Cover contents:

- feature article: photo of Paris Hilton with caption 'Dumped by Nicole now Mischa hates her too — Paris' secret heartache'
- advice on self-presentation and relationships: '289 flirty looks'
- puff: 'Britain's first interactive magazine — bliss world'
- advice on relationships: 'When will you pull *the one*? We know!'
- fashion advice: 'Ditch the tights and flash some flesh!'
- confession/true story: True crime special: 'I'm 16 and in jail for murdering mum' and 'Attacked in my bed by psycho stranger'
- makeover: 'Do you need a body makeover? Find out how your figure measures up'

Articles include:

- behind the scenes at Channel 4 soap: 'Hanging out with *Hollyoaks*'
- a global warming alert
- face and body worries
- horoscope
- problem pages
- confessions from readers
- articles on celebrities
- advice on relationships: 'fit lads' give their opinion on whether sexual experience matters in a girlfriend

Comment: the magazine's contents combine all the usual concerns of teenage girls with a glossy, sophisticated and contemporary adult feel. It is a lifestyle magazine where happiness involves relationships, consumption of goods and spending money on make-up, clothes, accessories, shoes and mobile phones. The usual insecurities of teenage life concerning personality and appearance and how to behave in relationships (evident in *Jackie* 30 years earlier) are still present beneath the sophisticated packaging, and 40% of *Bliss*'s young readers have considered plastic surgery.

EXAMINER'S TIP

The practical, handbag-sized A5 'baby glossy' format used by *Bliss* has proved to be increasingly popular since being pioneered by the highly successful *Glamour* magazine (publisher Condé Nast). Other magazines, including *Cosmopolitan*, now publish in A5 format.

TERMINOLOGY

Content analysis: this research technique involves the systematic analysis of the contents of a media product. Content analysis is in the empirical tradition and involves testing observable evidence, such as counting how often a particular element appears in a media product.

Men's magazines ('lads' mags')

The men's magazine market developed from the successful female lifestyle magazines in the 1970s, with *Cosmopolitan* having a 'Cosmo Men' section in recognition of the number of men reading the magazine.

Reasons for the development of lads' mags

- A gap in the market — young men with money to spend had no style magazines specifically directed at them.
- To meet advertisers' and product manufacturers' needs — the magazines are an ideal vehicle for targeting the lucrative market of young men, with advertisements for aftershave, watches, gadgets, cars, bikes, clothes, music, DVDs, computer games and alcohol.
- The top shelf problem — sexually explicit soft porn magazines aimed at young men were not wholesome enough to attract mainstream advertisers and were magazines to hide rather than to be seen with; they had no lifestyle marketing appeal to advertisers.
- The return of the 'pin-up' — the new generation of magazines offer teasing glamour rather than pornography.
- The new male consumer — market research shows young men to be spending more on clothes, appearance and lifestyle products, all of which could be built into the magazines' contents.
- More relaxed views on homosexuality make it easier for young men to buy magazines with a focus on lifestyle and looks without appearing less masculine.
- Male identity and the 'new lad' as a marketing tool — this follows talk of a crisis of male identity in the face of an increased cultural focus on the achievements and advancement of women.
- The magazines create role models and lifestyle options, built around the consumption of goods.

GQ (Gentleman's Quarterly)

Problems of gender identity and homophobic fears held back the launching of men's style magazines for several years. In 1987, *GQ* was launched by Condé Nast, with the first issue having a picture of Conservative politician and businessman Michael Heseltine on the cover. Early editions of the magazine continued to use male role model figures on the covers — for example, movie stars Gary Oldman, Jeff Bridges and Michael Douglas and television comedian Paul Whitehouse — to assert their masculinity and seriousness.

The magazine contains serious articles on topics of interest to the readership. From the mid-1990s, the magazine began to feature attractive semi-naked girls on the front cover, partly as a result of competition from *Loaded* and *FHM*.

Point for discusssion

In the 1980s, magazine publishers were concerned that magazines that relied on fashion spreads and aftershave adverts would attract a gay market and homophobic reactions from 'straight' males, while pin-ups of naked girls would place them in the 'top shelf' bracket of sex magazines such as *Playboy* and *Mayfair*. The development of lifestyle marketing and more tolerant and relaxed attitudes towards sexuality made it easier to market a new generation of men's magazine. The idea of a softer, less macho masculinity and the marketing by the media of the 'new man' who is not afraid to show feelings and emotions has played a significant part in the development of men's style magazines.

FHM, Maxim and Loaded

These glossy magazines, described as containing 'girls, entertainment, sport and stupid jokes', contain raunchy, irreverent articles, fashion spreads, partly-clothed pin-ups and features on holidays, alcohol, music, relationships, personal advice, cars, bikes, sport and entertainment, representing the lifestyle and interests of the 'new lad'. They are largely entertainment-based in content, but do include some articles and features on issues of cultural and social importance.

They are vehicles for advertisers, although many of their younger readers merely aspire to the cars, bikes, watches and other expensive consumer items advertised. Some of the back pages of the magazine are filled with small ads for sex chat lines and porno-graphic web sites. They contain sexualised images of semi-naked girls, who are often well known from soap operas or entertainment culture, and these idealised females represent the sexual aspirations of the readers.

The magazines attempt to define masculinity in the age of 'girl power' but have borrowed most of their style from women's magazines.

Point for discussion

The lads' and teenage girls' magazines tend to reinforce traditional gender roles and stereotypes. They assume that the principal interests of girls are personal appearance, clothes, make-up, sex, relationships and boyfriends. There is little on education and careers. Boys are assumed to be interested in expensive toys, sport, alcohol and sex — all of which can be bought through advertisements in the magazines. Remember, magazines deliver audiences to advertisers.

Questions to ask when analysing magazines
- Are readers being encouraged to identify with celebrities?
- Who are the people being represented in the magazine?
- Do the magazines reinforce negative stereotypes of young people?
- What kind of behaviour/lifestyle is being encouraged or endorsed?
- What kinds of activity are not included?
- Who does the lifestyle model benefit?
- Who is excluded from this lifestyle model?

- Month after month editions are very similar, so are the magazines anything more than advertising and marketing copy exploiting the insecurities of their readers for commercial gain?
- What percentage of the magazine is devoted to advertisements?

Why do girls buy magazines?

- The magazines offer escapism, and the chance to fantasise about the lives and loves of celebrities.
- Depression — a magazine cheers them up and suggests ways in which they can change themselves and their appearance.
- Gossip and curiosity — girls like to read stories about the behaviour of others.
- Romance — magazines give them ideas about how to attract the opposite sex.
- Affiliation needs — reading the magazines makes them feel part of an exciting world.

Why do lads buy magazines?

- The magazines offer escapism.
- They contain pictures of half-naked girls, who are presented as idealised girlfriends.
- Jokes and stories about sex and outrageous behaviour appeal to young men.
- Music and entertainment reviews, sports coverage and pictures of desirable cars, bikes, watches, clothes and other consumer items tie in with aspirations of the readers.
- Affiliation needs — there is a desire among readers to be 'one of the lads'.

EXAMINER'S TIP

Remember that magazine producers want their magazines to become embedded in the everyday lives of their readers. All magazines operate websites that further entice and engage their audience. These offer access to merchandise and further develop the magazine's contents; they also offer online dating, which enhances their matchmaking role.